THROUGH THE
FIRES

*An American Business Story
of Turbulence, Triumph
and Giving Back*

ROBERT OWEN CARR
WITH DIRK JOHNSON

Through the Fires: An American Business Story
of Turbulence, Triumph and Giving Back

Printed in the United States of America

ISBN 978-0-9909386-0-6 (hardcover)

This book is dedicated to

Mary Frances Carr

*Corrie, Jeff, Jessica, Jake, Bob, Melissa, Ava, Ryan,
Holly, Ryan, Kelly and Emmalee*

Don Lassiter

Larry Schiffer, Bob Niehaus and Mitchell Hollin

TABLE OF CONTENTS

PREFACE

On these pages, I share some moments of my own struggle, as well as my good fortune, in the spirit of helping a bit by giving back.

I am a lucky man.

While I have faced some nasty setbacks and disappointments, in life and work, I recognize that many people have navigated a much rockier road than I have ever known. Their resilience is an inspiration.

I was blessed to have a mother who was loving, present and thoughtful. I had a seventh-grade teacher who changed my life by convincing me that it would be all right to go to college after all, despite the views of my parents. He convinced me that I should prepare a backup plan for my life, just in case my dream of playing second base for the Chicago White Sox didn't work out.

I succeeded with business partners and colleagues, directors, friends, family and employees who stood beside me with energy, wisdom and loyalty. And I relied, in the most difficult times, on the last soul to stay with me in the darkest of times, Don Lassiter.

Timing, too, has been on my side. I entered graduate school just as the career of computer programming was blossoming. I worked in a world that was transformed and enriched by the powers of increasingly sophisticated technology. I benefited from the ingenious work of Bill Gates and Steve Jobs, and so many other pioneers of the computer and business worlds. I worked with payment industry giants who created the plastic world that has helped so many businesses and consumers.

I watched each step of the way as the power of a mainframe computer was gradually dwarfed by the power of the minicomputer and then the microcomputer, and now the smartphone. As Heartland was formed, I was helped by brilliant financial friends and advisers who believed in me—in good times and bad.

I have been given robust health, while so many others suffered maladies or whose time was cut short.

I revel in the greatest of gifts—brilliant and caring children— six individuals who are so special that it makes clear to me that nature trumps nurture. I have surely learned from them more than I have taught. And my four grandchildren fill me with wonder and awe.

For those young people who feel rejection, for the business person who is trying yet again to solve the riddle, for those who watch unpaid bills stacking up, for people who consider giving up the fight, for those outraged at the unfairness of the system, and for those who want to fix a little bit of what is wrong with this world, this is a story of kinship, humility and possibility.

ROBERT OWEN CARR

1

SURVIVING A PUNCH

It was Easter Sunday in 1959, the golden era of American wholesomeness and family values. I was thirteen years old, sitting in the front seat of the Ford Fairlane alongside my dad. It was the only car in the parking lot of Corwin's Pharmacy in Lockport, Illinois.

And I was holding up my arms to fend off the flogging blows from my father's hands.

You're a sissy, he sneered. *I'm going to make you into a man. You are a sissy. You won't even fight back.*

Easter was the only day of the year that my father attended church, and only then because my mother pleaded and begged.

The Carr family had sat in the pews of the First Congregational Church of Lockport. I stood sheepishly behind the altar. I was a member of the choir.

I had joined the group as a favor to my mother, Mary. She was a woman who blistered her feet waitressing in the evenings at a restaurant, while my dad ran around with other women, or stayed home and drowned himself in beer and bourbon.

If joining the choir would please my mother, it was reason enough.

On most Sundays, two other boys sang in the choir. But neither had showed up that morning.

In the pew, my father sat and fumed.

After the services, we drove back home to our house in the country, seven miles outside Lockport, a rural section known as Homer. Our home sat across the road from a house where our neighbors raised chickens. Next to them was another neighbor whose pigs sometimes crossed over to our yard and got wrapped up in the clothes hanging on the line.

When we arrived at home, my dad told me to stay in the car. He said we needed to go for a ride, just the two of us.

We were going to have a *man-to-man* talk.

He steered the car into the parking lot of Corwin's. In those days, the stores all closed on Sundays. The lot would be empty. No one would be around to see us.

In a voice simmering with rage, he told me that I had humiliated him—the only boy in a choir full of girls. It was too much for his pride to bear.

He drew back his arm and began to swing.

In my short life, I had tried very hard to win my father's approval. My dad wanted me to be more like my older brother, Bill, the biggest kid in his class—athletic, smart and *tough*.

When my dad worked on the car, I would stand for hours at his side, holding the tools or pointing the flashlight. When I played ball games at family gatherings, I looked to see if he was watching.

I had long hoped for my dad to be proud of me.

On that Easter Sunday in the parking lot of Corwin's, I gave up hoping.

To Arthur Charles Carr, I wasn't even worth the time or money to take to the doctor.

When I had just turned sixteen, my hand was caught in a slamming steel door at Lockport Township High School. The middle finger on my right hand had been crushed.

My dad looked at it for an instant before scoffing:

This happens all the time to men! You will get over it! Shake it off!

As the days passed, my finger turned darker and darker. I was developing gangrene. My mother, in defiance of my father's objections, took me to the emergency room at Silver Cross Hospital in Joliet.

The doctors were outraged. *Why had this kid gone untreated? Gangrene can kill.*

I was put under anesthesia and taken into surgery where they worked to cleanse the infection, scrape the bone, and cut off the diseased flesh in the top digit of my finger.

The injury meant I could not take the test for a driver's license until well past my sixteenth birthday. In those days, getting your license was just about the biggest deal in the life of an adolescent. I ended up being the last kid in my class to take the driving test. I flunked it.

When I took the test again, my dad laughed that he had never heard of anyone who didn't get their driver's license until they were seventeen.

To this day, when I look at my finger, I think of my father.

More than once in my life, I have known failure.

Ambitious business ideas have fallen short. Unpaid bills have piled up. Credit cards have been canceled. Bill collectors have come after me for house payments.

In 1976, newly divorced, broke and alone, I moved back to my hometown in Illinois. Trying to survive in my business as a software and business consultant, I lived and worked in the dreary Lockport South Apartments and then moved to East Street.

I walked out of my building on East Street early one day to see a tow truck lifting the rear end of my car. Somehow I was able to beg the repo man into letting me keep my lime green Pontiac.

Years down the road, living in Florida and searching for success, the bills still outran me. With the mortgage past due, I was served an order of foreclosure: *Get out of the house by Tuesday—or expect the sheriff's deputy to break into your house and put your furniture on the street.*

．．．

On August 11, 2005, I stood on the floor of the New York Stock Exchange.

Congratulations, said the chief executive of the exchange, John Thain, thrusting his hand for a shake. *This must be a very happy day for you.*

I had rung the bell at 9:30 a.m. to open trading. My company, Heartland Payment Systems, had gone public on that day.

Demand was so great that the stock was oversubscribed by twenty-two times. In other words, for every share that was issued, there were twenty-two orders. My banker told me it was the most successful initial public offering in the history of the payments industry, breaking a record set by PayPal.

The stock price climbed so furiously that the company's value increased more than $100 million on that first day.

Heartland Payment Systems (HPY), which I have led as chairman and chief executive officer since its inception, processes debit and credit card transactions. When a card is swiped, we electronically link the customer, the business, the bank and the card brand, such as Visa or MasterCard—all in little more than the blink of an eye.

The company was worth $2 million when it was founded in 1997. It has since grown to a market capitalization of more than $1.8 billion.

But even after the successful launch of the company, adversity lurked. In 2009, Heartland would face a terrifying disaster, an ordeal that threatened to close our company and leave me in financial ruin at age sixty-three.

. . .

When you've been knocked down in life or business, time and again, how do you get up?

How do you survive failure, sustain your confidence and keep pressing ahead?

What do you use as a compass?

I happen to be an amateur student of baseball and presidents. I've been to forty-seven major league ballparks and all fifty state capitals. I've visited the birthplaces and tombs of almost all of our late presidents.

I like to think I've learned something about enduring a loss, dusting myself off, and coming back.

President Calvin Coolidge was famous for not saying much. Upon the passing of Silent Cal, the brilliantly sardonic writer, Dorothy Parker, was said to have remarked: *How could they tell?*

But Coolidge hit the spot with this observation:

Nothing in the world can take the place of persistence. Talent will not; nothing is more common than unsuccessful men with talent. Genius will not; unrewarded genius is almost a proverb. Education will not; the world is full of educated derelicts. Persistence and determination alone are omnipotent.

When I was twenty, as I reflected on my father's life and choices, I asked myself a simple question:

At the age of sixty, if I am lucky enough to grow that old, will I be proud of the life I have led? Will I have made a difference—a positive one?

I've learned this much. The right thing to do, it seems to me, is to try to do the right thing. But it is no guarantee for success. The sad truth is that too often crime does pay. Plenty of villains scheme all the way to the bank. And the claim of the old Brooklyn Dodger manager, Leo Durocher—*Nice guys finish last*—is right more often than it should be.

In corporate life, I have seen it plenty of times. Street toughs often wind up in the slammer, but white-collar pirates, the clever bandits with plenty of money for lawyers, tend to skate with impunity. Even worse are those highly educated tricksters who abuse the under-informed consumers and small business owners with outrageous and deceptive acts devised for the sole purpose of transferring money out of the bank accounts of the poor, with little or no value provided.

I've seen it in my industry, where too many unscrupulous companies take advantage of naive or overwhelmed small business people. The schemers thrive, and then brag about their cleverness.

It doesn't have to be this way.

. . .

Real character is revealed when people have no money or power, but also when they have a lot of it.

I have known both circumstances.

Mine is not the story you hear these days about tech geeks who become gazillionaires when they're so young they're still getting carded at bars.

At age fifty, I still didn't know if I was ever going to be financially solvent or not.

It is not easy to take the longer, circuitous path in search of career success, wondering if you will ever find your way out of the woods.

But you do gain some perspective from the experience. In particular, you develop an understanding for people who struggle. You see colleagues and customers in a different light when you know from experience what it's like to be unable to pay the bills.

There is not a whole lot of empathy for customers and middle managers and lower-level employees in many C-suites of corporate America today. In the view of some bottom-liners, it's a sign of weakness to let compassion or kindness shape leadership style or management decisions.

When you get right down to it, though, a CEO who is hugely successful, but who cheats, belittles or bullies the vulnerable, is really not much more than a better-dressed version of my dad—worse, in fact, because my dad at least was not a cold-blooded thief.

In September of 1963, I arrived at the University of Illinois, the Big Ten school that straddles Champaign and Urbana, surrounded by a sea of corn and soybean fields. It was the first time I had ever set foot on a campus.

I was grateful to be at the U of I, and fully aware that I would need to work hard to compete academically. In those days, about half of the freshman students would flunk out.

Because I scored well on the college entrance exam, the state of Illinois waived the $135 per semester tuition charge. But I still needed to pay for room and board. Earning ninety cents an hour at my job washing dishes at the university, I would need to work a whole lot.

I was in a terrible hurry. I grew determined to graduate in less than four years. To do that, I had to choose my classes with efficiency and economy in mind.

A wide range of subjects appealed to me: history, philosophy, literature, math, botany, geology, German. But with a work schedule of twenty-five hours a week, I based my choice of a major on a single fundamental standard: whatever subject would take the least amount of time.

Before registering for classes, I walked through the aisles of the college bookstore to survey the possibilities. I measured the various texts.

The math textbooks were the skinniest and math was my strongest area on the ACT. That settled it. I declared myself a math major.

And so, the sprint was on—in just about every way. I graduated with honors in three years with a bachelor's degree in math. Between my second and third year, I married my high school sweetheart, Susan. In my fourth year, I earned a master's degree in computer science while working as a manager at Arby's.

My graduate program at Illinois was among the first master's degree curricula in computer science in the nation. It was math and electrical engineering, with a little bit of computer programming thrown into the mix. In those days, that was enough for the school to package and market it as a hot new degree in an emerging field.

It worked.

After graduation, I applied for a job at a new community college in Champaign called Parkland College. The computer science degree, it turned out, was a ticket to ride.

I was offered a teaching job, and within a few months, I was made the director of the computer center. The next semester, I was elected president of the faculty organization. I was twenty-two years old and I was on a roll.

After doing some computer consulting work for the local CBS television station, I was offered a relatively big job at the Bank of Illinois in Champaign, and I took it, while keeping my position at Parkland.

Between the jobs, I was making $30,000. In the late '60s, that was ridiculous money for a kid barely out of college.

The Vietnam war was raging, and campuses everywhere were in turmoil. There had been protests in Champaign and gunshots were fired one night through the front windows of the bank.

I had been inspired by the election of John F. Kennedy, but I really came to revere his brother, Bobby. On the June night that RFK was assassinated at the Ambassador Hotel in Los Angeles, I watched the television reports, and I cried.

Like a lot of young people at the time, I wanted to solve the world's big problems. The independent path appealed to me. I was going to be my own man.

I had entered college with the intention of becoming a high school math teacher. But my ambitions had now grown much bigger.

At age twenty-five, I took out an advertisement that ran at the bottom of page 28 in the November 5, 1971, edition of the *New York Times*.

I was declaring a run for the White House.

Robert Owen Carr, 1429 Mayfair Road, Champaign, Illinois, 61820, hereby announces his intention to win the election twenty-five years from today for the presidency of the United States.

In the ad, I announced that my long campaign *begins today* and promised to *result in the election of the first independent president.*

It concluded, *Write for more information.*

I had vowed to refuse campaign contributions because I believed they corrupted the system. To self-finance my far-flung presidential campaign, I knew I would need to make a whole lot of money.

Less than two months later, with aspirations the size of Texas and a head almost as big, I quit both of my jobs.

I had decided to become an entrepreneur. I had $10,000 in the bank. I was smart, with a master's degree in computer science. I had experience in the banking world. And I had made business connections in Champaign.

Given a chance and the time, I believed, I could persuade almost anyone to my way of thinking. I was *certain* I would be lining up plenty of lucrative work as a consultant.

I did not consider the possibility that my business and personal life were headed for a very long and painful slide.

But that is precisely what would happen.

My wife, Susan, was less than thrilled with the career change. We had started our marriage in a tiny apartment on Fourth Street in Champaign, next to Boneyard Creek. When it turned cold, mice scurried into the kitchen. Susan stood on a chair and screamed. I carried her outside, and she never stepped inside the apartment again.

We moved to a $50-a-month house trailer, where the wind blew through the rickety walls and our bed was sometimes dusted with snow when we woke. We drove an old beater, a 1959 Volkswagen Beetle.

In the next four years, with my two degrees and my salaries from Parkland and the bank, we ascended to a comfortable life in a handsome three-bedroom ranch house near the Champaign Country Club. We were awfully young to be living in such a spiffy neighborhood.

People who rang the front doorbell would sometimes ask, *Are your parents home?*

We were all grown up, or so we thought. In July of 1970, we adopted a baby girl, Corrie. Eight months later, Susan was pregnant with Bob, Jr.

After I struck out on my own, charging toward an uncertain future, Susan grew disenchanted, and then disapproving. As a fledgling entrepreneur, I worked hard for big success, but often came up empty. In 1975, she finally gave up on me. We separated the following year. Our third child, Holly, had not yet been born.

. . .

For years, I would bounce around the country: Tennessee, Oklahoma, Florida, New Jersey, with two stints back in Lockport. At one point, I was driving seventeen hours each way between Illinois and the panhandle of Oklahoma. This was a land of scattered sagebrush and wandering cattle, and a lot of oil and gas. It was dubbed *No Man's Land*. Trying to eke out a living and build a great business, I stayed in cheap hotels or bunked at the homes of clients.

I married Jill Jackson in 1980. Jill convinced me that we might as well move to Oklahoma, since I was spending most of my time there.

We settled in Beaver, a little town that proudly billed itself as the *Cow Chip Throwing Capital of the World*. I bought Jill a Ford Escort, and on the first night, it was coated in brown dirt after a rainstorm. That's how much dust was in the air.

In the coming years, we would have three children: Ryan, Kelly and Emmalee.

It was in the lonely Oklahoma country that I would make an important technological breakthrough. I was working with a company called Dace Oil, a small jobber that supplied fuel and oil from Phillips 66 to truckers, ranchers, farmers, gas stations and convenience stores. Dace had an unattended fueling station. Truckers would pull up to a pump to refuel any time of the day or night.

Each of these drivers had a white plastic card with punched holes. It was the kind of card that hotel and motel chains used as room keys years ago. When the truckers inserted the cards, the purchases were recorded electronically in a little electronic box near the pump.

I saw an opportunity. I wrote software that would electronically transport those transactions into a personal computer, which had been programmed with software I had coded and integrated into a series of programs that I had written for the new PCs.

I didn't invent pay-at-the-pump transactions. I wish I had. But this was the first time that such transactions were processed by a microcomputer. My integrated software packages ran on Bill Gates' new DOS operating systems. In later years, QuickBooks and Intuit were smart enough to make a multibillion-dollar business out of what I was trying to create in the late '70s and early '80s.

The search for success took Jill and me to Florida in 1986. I had been given a chance to run a payment processing company that served accounts like 7-11 stores across the state. What made the position especially appealing was a 25 percent ownership share in the company.

When I was recruited, I had been told there was no debt. As soon as I arrived, however, I learned the company owed more than $1 million.

It was time to try again. I started my own company in 1987— Credit Card Software Systems. In the beginning I had two partners, but they quickly disappeared, certain that the company was going nowhere.

A plain-spoken North Carolinian, Don Lassiter, stuck with me. And then just as we were finding our legs as a viable company, in January of 1990, we were hit with a fraud that cost us $90,000. We didn't have that kind of money, and it looked for a time like Jill and I were going to lose our house.

In an act of kindness I will never forget, Don agreed to work in sales for a year with no salary or compensation of any kind, living off the $70,000 he had received from the sale of his tractors and other farm equipment. In exchange, I promised to give him a share of the company, equal to 40 percent of what I then owned—once we hit it big.

With a lot of hard work, one sale turned into another, and our business grew stable. Jill and I moved again in 1992, this time to New Jersey. We had found a good school in Princeton for our little ones. We rented a house, which we eventually bought on contract, and used the basement for an office.

We had finally prospered enough to start paying ourselves livable salaries, when some unexpected visitors came knocking. It was the original partners, sniffing a chance to capitalize on our success. One of them had inserted a clause in our original contract—a stipulation I had misjudged—giving him control of the company in the event of a breakup. He went to arbitration and cut me out of the business.

I was broke again.

Angry and disheartened, but vowing to climb the hill once again, Don and I started another company, which we called Omnicard. Before long, every one of our former partner's employees left him and came to work for our new enterprise.

With our promising business model, I met in November of 1996 with the chairman of the board of Heartland Bank, Larry Schiffer, a man introduced to me through a mutual friend. By the time we finished dinner, Larry agreed on a partnership that established Heartland Payment Systems. Within ten days, he gave me a loan for $100,000. I needed it. I had gone without any income for more than six months.

We soon opened a 2,100-square-foot office on the third floor of Heartland Bank's headquarters in Clayton, Missouri. We grew so rapidly that we could scarcely keep pace with demand, and then moved to nearby quarters that were five times bigger. By the end of March 1998, we were processing 1,000 new customer contracts a month.

In 2001, with business exploding, we sold about 50 percent of our company to Wall Street investors, Greenhill Capital and LLR Partners, for $40 million.

At the age of fifty-five, after all the heartache and struggle, I had become a wealthy man.

And so did Don.

I kept the promise to give him an ownership share. On the day Heartland went public, Don ended up with stock worth more than $35 million. It is now valued at more than $80 million. In our business dealings, Don and I had never exchanged a single piece of paper. It had simply been a handshake.

Flush for the first time in our lives, Jill and I purchased President Woodrow Wilson's old house in 2003. It was a Tudor style on Library Place in Princeton that Wilson and his wife, Ellen, had designed and built in 1896 when he was a professor at the Ivy League school. I long ago had given up the idea of ever being president, but now I was able to live in the home designed and built by one of the most influential presidents in American history.

The company continued to flourish. Among financial processors, Heartland quickly grew from the sixty-second in size to the sixth largest by 2005.

In October of that heady year, I took a big crew of family and friends to watch my beloved Chicago White Sox play in the World Series. As a little boy, I lived for the Sox. For many of the years of my childhood, we didn't have a television, and we didn't get a newspaper.

So I would rise very early—before anybody was awake— and skip across the road to the house where the chickens were squawking. The neighbors had the *Chicago Tribune* delivered into one of those plastic tubes near our mailbox.

Careful not to make any noise, I would step quietly and open their newspaper and devour every word about the Sox, and then put the paper back in the tube.

Now here I was at the ballpark, a successful CEO of a thriving company. My Sox were in the Series, *and I was sitting with my family behind the dugout!*

And then off we flew to Las Vegas for our yearly company gathering. We usually held the conference in Louisville, Kentucky, across the Ohio River from our service center in

Jeffersonville, Indiana. But this year was special. We had gone big time. And we were going to celebrate in style.

Heartland had some 1,800 employees by then. We footed the bill for many of the workers to come to the new Paris Hotel on the Strip. We did some business. And the champagne flowed.

During that autumn, Jill and I bought a lovely lake house in New Hampshire, and later acquired one-hundred wooded acres nearby to preserve the land from development.

We took a trip to Monaco for our twenty-fifth anniversary, a paradise that neither of us working-class Lockport kids had even dreamed about. We stayed in a resort on the Mediterranean Sea. On a lark, we looked at some yachts that were for sale.

A skeptical broker asked some questions, just to make sure we had real money.

It won't be a problem, I assured him.

Some of these nautical masterpieces were priced at $30 million or more. We looked at a former British naval ship with marble bathrooms. When you buy a yacht, it needs year-round upkeep. We were told the floral arrangements alone would cost $2,000 a week.

We did not buy the flowers, or the yacht.

The yearly tab for the flowers alone, it dawned on me, would be enough to put some kids through four years of college.

That hit close to home.

I had established the *Give Something Back Foundation*, which awards scholarships to poor and working-class kids. It was my way of returning the favor for a $250 award I had received from the Lockport Woman's Club when I was a senior in high school. I have set a goal of sending at least 1,000 disadvantaged kids through college.

It was time to pay back, since everything seemed to be going my way. Ernst and Young named me the Entrepreneur of the Year in the financial services category, and honored me a second time for my foundation work. The Greater Philadelphia Chamber of Commerce recognized me as the top entrepreneur. Our industry trade group gave me its inaugural Lifetime Achievement Award. The *Wall Street Journal* wrote a very flattering article about Heartland and the company's unusual and generous compensation program for employees.

My net worth grew to more than $300 million in Heartland stock. I believed that I could become a billionaire. Our stock had gone from thirty cents to $33 per share in seven years. Why wouldn't it go to $100?

I envisioned my name listed among the titans of the *Forbes* 400.

On January 12, 2009, after a day of meetings in New York, I was having dinner at the Blue Fin on Broadway with my colleague, Bob Baldwin, who at the time was the president and chief financial officer at Heartland. We had spent that day with investment bankers, exploring the possibility of buying a bank.

After a gin and tonic, I made the short walk back to the Crowne Plaza Hotel through the neon glitz of Times Square.

When I arrived, I discovered an urgent message. I was to call our head of technology in Plano, Texas. According to the message, it was an extremely serious matter.

When I called the tech chief, his voice was grave.

We have definite evidence of a breach.

He told Baldwin and me that files with vast amounts of data, not created by Heartland, had been discovered in our system. We had been attacked and infiltrated on a devastating scale.

It was soon described as the largest security breach in history. Credit and debit card numbers—and information for millions of transactions—could have been exposed. As bad as it is for a retailer like Home Depot or Target or Neiman Marcus to be hit with a breach, it is potentially even more damaging, and damning, when it happens to a transactions company with its access to so many cards and a promise to protect them.

This was a catastrophe. I knew immediately it could mean the end of Heartland.

That night, I lay awake in my hotel room. I am not a man who stares at the bedroom ceiling. But I did not sleep an hour that night.

I shed some tears.

After all those years of struggle, I had proved that my ideas of building a successful business could work and work big. I had helped build something pretty amazing,

Now it could all be gone.

2

THE CLOCK IS TICKING

We called federal law enforcement authorities. We informed our company's board of directors. We alerted Visa, MasterCard, American Express and Discover. We consulted with lawyers. We hired a crisis management firm.

Looking for advice, and perhaps a measure of empathy, I called the former CEO of Johnson & Johnson, who had endured a famous tampering crisis with Tylenol in the early 1980s.

We wanted to do the right thing.

But what exactly *was* the right thing?

That was a matter of opinion.

Companies up until that time would provide only the minimum information required by law. We had reported the matter to the authorities and we were cooperating. We would file the required disclosure known as an 8-K about the breach with the Securities and Exchange Commission. We had no legal obligation to do anything more than that.

I believed strongly, however, that we needed to be more forthcoming. We needed to issue an official statement going beyond the 8-K and talk to our employees and customers and the rest of our shareholders. I wanted to be open about the breach, own up to it, whatever the consequences. I trusted that our employees and our reputation as a forthright company with integrity would carry the day.

I was sitting in a room full of lawyers. One of them spoke up. His tone was ominous. He said they were just trying to protect me from myself.

Bob, if you go public with this and say the wrong things, you might wind up going to jail, he warned. *We want to keep that from happening.*

I fired back.

What in the hell are you talking about?

He pretty much explained that I might not know when to keep my mouth shut. An aggressive prosecutor might catch me in an innocent misstatement and nail me for some violation.

But we have done nothing wrong, I said. *I have done nothing wrong. I am not going to dodge the truth.*

I told him he was acting like an undertaker trying to put lipstick on a corpse.

We aren't dead yet, I told him.

When it came to manipulation, this lawyer was an amateur compared to my dad. I had sworn decades ago that I would never cave to a bully again. I was not going to start now.

With my intentions firm, I met on Friday, January 16, with the inner circle of Heartland leaders to discuss implementing the next steps. I huddled with Baldwin, Nancy Gross, our chief marketing officer, and Charles Kallenbach, our chief legal counsel.

Charles was to draft a news release and the 8-K about the breach over the weekend.

The following Monday was the Martin Luther King holiday, so the markets would be closed. The next trading day was Tuesday, January 20. It was Inauguration Day, an especially historic day for the country, as Barack Obama would be taking the oath as the first African American president.

It was our plan to issue the statement on Tuesday morning, at least two hours before the markets opened.

We expected a thunderous storm over the news, and a damaging hit to the stock price. After being shocked by news of the breach, I had shifted my mission to doing everything I could to save 2,500 jobs, to protect our 150,000 customers, and to keep Heartland alive.

My father had unwittingly trained me well at a very early age to successfully navigate choppy waters.

To divide responsibilities, we decided that Bob Baldwin would handle inquiries from the media and investors. I would talk to employees and customers.

I walked home that Friday afternoon and retreated to my dark oak-paneled library that I had designed to look like my remembrance of the University of Illinois math library, where I had spent so many hours.

The markets closed at 4 p.m. At 4:01 p.m., I started making phone calls. I called about forty people, including each of my six children. My kids asked questions about the bad guys who had stolen credit card numbers from the company. They asked if we would be able to catch the criminals. Mostly they wanted to know if I was going to be okay.

I reached out to Don Lassiter. He had stuck with me in two of our darkest periods in the '90s. I had even told him years before that I might need to give up on my dreams of being a successful entrepreneur.

Back in those difficult days, Don had convinced me to hang in there, keep pressing ahead. He believed in our business model and he believed in me, and so I took a leap of faith. Without Don, there would have been no Heartland.

He had retired by the time of the breach. When I called, he heard the gravity in my voice. Don would later say he thought I was going to tell him that I was dying. As he would learn, it was the death of the company that I feared.

On Monday morning, the Heartland leaders huddled. I thought we were all on the same page about the way to proceed. I would find out differently.

Over the weekend, they had met in Philadelphia with the crisis advisers while I was on the phone in Princeton. The message from all the experts: Make the required disclosure to the SEC, *but say nothing more* to the public, employees, customers, and stockholders. Say only the absolute minimum about the breach.

From my perspective, this was 180 degrees from our agreement on the previous Friday. They had met with the outside experts and the message from the advisers was intense and relentless: Provide only the minimum information in the public statement.

As these experts noted, we were perfectly within our legal rights. Virtually all companies would handle it the same way.

The outside lawyers had raised grave concerns. They told my team that disclosing more than what was legally required meant courting great risk. If we bit our tongues and hung on tight, we might be able to weather the storm. If we said too much, it could very well mean the end of the company.

They talked again about the potential for criminal charges and jail time. That was damned intimidating.

While we knew we had done nothing wrong, these outside lawyers couldn't be sure of that. They said it was better to play it safe.

My Heartland colleagues had the best of intentions. They only wanted what was best for the company. They were justifiably scared. They came to the conclusion that these experts must be right.

When we gathered on Monday morning, they tried to convince me to change my mind.

I felt betrayed.

This raised a serious ethical issue. We had a corporate culture at stake. All along, we've been saying that we were a different kind of company. And we had *behaved* like a different kind of company.

But when we are faced with trouble, I challenged my leadership team, are we just going to duck and dive like everybody else?

And what will happen if we are silent about this when asked questions or invited to speak? How would our customers and employees ever trust us again if we clammed up and said, in effect, '*The lawyers told us not to say anything*'?

How does our brand and reputation for transparency survive by disclosing only the bare minimum about a disastrous breach?

The others didn't see it that way. They thought I was being stubborn, even self-righteous.

They insisted that we had a responsibility to do what was best and safest for the company. We were paying for the advice of specialists in crisis, and they were warning against talking about the breach. As stewards of the company, didn't we have an obligation to follow the advice of the experts?

The atmosphere was boiling. We shouted at one another. We begged.

We got nowhere.

We agreed to meet again on Tuesday at 6:30 a.m. We were inching perilously close to the deadline for making the biggest career decision of our lives.

Before dawn, I drank a cup of strong coffee, walked out of Woodrow Wilson's front door and made my way toward the Heartland headquarters six blocks away. I knew it would be one of the most important days of my life.

If our earlier meeting had been angry, this one was even more impassioned. And the clock was ticking.

We argued until 7 a.m., and we kept arguing. At 7:25 a.m., I stood up.

I appreciate your position, I told them, my voice rising, and then turned squarely to our chief counsel. *As the CEO, I am directing you, Charles, to send the announcement to the New York Stock Exchange now. That's an order.*

My colleagues walked out of my office.

I sat alone.

Later, I took a walk down the hallway. As I passed Charles' office, I saw our dedicated corporate lawyer sitting at his desk. He had filed the release. A few tears were running down his cheeks. I suspect that he wasn't the only one who shed tears that day.

The release was topped with a headline: *Heartland Payment Systems Uncovers Malicious Software in Its Processing System.*

We explained that the security breach appeared to be the work of a widespread global cyber fraud operation. We announced that Heartland would implement a next-generation program designed to flag network anomalies in real time.

We also created a website—www.2008breach.com—to provide information about the incident. We advised cardholders to examine their monthly statements and report any suspicious activity to their card issuers. We emphasized that cardholders were not responsible for unauthorized fraudulent charges made by third parties.

As soon as the announcement was made, the telephone started ringing.

The same release had gone out to our staff, and at 9 a.m., I conducted a conference call with our 2,500 employees.

I did not mince words. I told them that this was bad, very bad. It could seriously damage the company.

I wanted them to hear it from me—not from the media, or anybody else.

Your mission after this phone call, I told them, *is to go out and talk to your customers.*

I wanted the customers to learn about the breach from us. Let them know that none of their store information had been compromised. Their customers would lose no money. They would be made whole for any fraudulent activity.

At 11 a.m., a reporter, Brian Krebs, from the *Washington Post*, called and talked to Bob Baldwin. An article was soon posted describing the breach as the largest in history. A story about the crisis at Heartland was broadcast on the CBS Evening News.

From my office, I look directly at Nassau Hall, the heart of Princeton University, which served briefly as the United States Capitol building in 1783. It was in Old Nassau that George Washington and the Continental Congress had been headquartered.

I walked home before noon and passed the Princeton Borough Hall, as I did every day. I looked in admiration at the bust of Albert Einstein in EMC Square. Then I walked past the Princeton Battle Monument showing George Washington on horseback—the monument that commemorated the famous Battle of Princeton.

When I arrived home, I sat down in front of the television to watch President Obama address the nation. He had announced his candidacy on the steps of the old Illinois State House in Springfield, a place that evoked memories of Abraham Lincoln, the Great Emancipator.

It was Lincoln who had helped convince the Illinois legislature to found my hometown of Lockport. In the next weeks, on Lincoln's 200th birthday, I was scheduled to be dedicating a new park, Lincoln Landing, at the site of the Illinois and Michigan Canal in Lockport. It was important to me that people in my hometown, especially the kids, knew that our little town had played a significant role in history. To build the park, my foundation had spent $5 million, money that I had borrowed against my now-imperiled stock holdings.

As I watched the new president on my television, Obama spoke of trying times.

Today I say to you that the challenges we face are real. They are serious and they are many. They will not be met easily or in a short span of time. But know this, America: They will be met.

For Heartland, and for me, personally, I knew the road ahead would be rough. But we were determined not to lose our spirit. Our challenges, indeed, were many. And they would be met.

When I walked back to the office, my phone was ringing. One employee after the next was calling to say they were proud that we had gone public and were telling the truth about the breach.

Our people were determined to do whatever it took to ensure the survival of the company. The Heartland family was rallying. There were repeated expressions of unity, a kind of *us-against-the-world* togetherness. In some very important ways, we had become stronger than ever.

In our moment of crisis, I was grateful to be a Heartlander. But I also recognized that if the stock crashed too badly, my margin loans—borrowed primarily for college scholarships and Lincoln Landing—might wipe out my fortune.

. . .

In the wake of the Lehman and AIG scandals, and the overall economic collapse, Heartland stock had already fallen from a high of $33 to just under $16. Now after the breach, Heartland stock would lose nearly half its value once again, in a matter of days, with the price dipping to a little over $8.

Heartland's stock—HPY, dubbed *happy* by John Thain, CEO of the NYSE, for its ticker symbol—continued to drop for weeks. My ownership of Heartland stock was in mortal danger.

I am a risk-taker. Like a lot of entrepreneurs, it's the way I'm wired. But this had not been a reckless bet. I had watched the company grow exponentially. And we were getting stronger. That's why I didn't want to sell my stock, and decided instead to borrow against it. I had the option to borrow up to forty percent of the value, but I was being careful, and borrowed only ten percent.

My margins were extremely comfortable. Or so it seemed.

As the stock price dipped lower and lower, I soon recognized that all of my personal wealth might disappear.

My broker called on a Sunday night in early March. His voice was full of resignation.

I'm sorry, he told me. *We're going to have to sell your shares. There's nothing we can do about it.*

My Heartland stock was sold for just $3.45 a share to pay the margin loans. I even had to borrow 500,000 shares from the trusts of my children to completely pay off the margin loan.

I had taken a risk and lost. I had been worth $330 million— and now it was gone. I had been the largest stockholder in the company—and now I did not own a single share.

People sometimes find this hard to believe, but I didn't experience the loss of a financial fortune as cataclysmic. I did not shed a tear.

There are worse things that can happen to you than losing all of your money. One of them would be losing your self-respect.

At the time we learned about the breach, we could not have known that the bad guy had already been captured.

And there was a shocking twist.

The leader of the crew of cyberthieves in the Heartland breach was being paid a salary by the United States Secret Service.

Albert Gonzalez was drawing $75,000 a year to work as an undercover informant in a campaign to combat cyber fraud.

The authorities did not know that Gonzalez was working both sides of the street.

American Greed, a television show on CNBC, would later describe the twenty-six-year-old community college dropout as the mastermind of an international scheme and *the most cunning cyber crook* in the nation's history.

Gonzalez had grown up in Miami, the son of boat refugees from Cuba. As a child, he had displayed an obsession for computers. In high school, he used a library computer to hack into a site run by the government of India. He was not charged in the case. Instead, he was warned to stay away from computers for six months.

He graduated from South Miami High School in 1999. He enrolled in Dade Community College, but left after a single semester.

He moved to New York City and worked briefly for a company in its information technology department. Police say he did some drug dealing, and then soon drifted to Kearney, New Jersey, and began a career in cyber theft.

He became the administrator of a web site called *ShadowCrew*, which trafficked in stolen credit card numbers. He went by various handles, including *CumbaJohnny*.

Long before the breach, police had arrested Gonzalez in 2003 in New York City, when they found him standing at an ATM, illegally withdrawing money from an account that did not belong to him.

When law enforcement authorities discovered that he was CumbaJohnny, the guy who ran the ShadowCrew criminal site, they put aside the charges in exchange for cooperation.

They gave him a job as a snitch for the Secret Service, and he worked in a takedown called *Operation Firewall*, a 2004 sting that netted 28 arrests.

Gonzalez returned to Miami, still on the government payroll, continuing to send tips to the Secret Service.

But he was also going into business for himself. Gonzalez recruited a pack of computer nerds and became their leader in cyber theft. They called their enterprise, *Operation Get Rich or Die Tryin'*.

He and his accomplices would cruise U.S. Highway 1 in Miami on missions called *War Drives*. Using a Wi-Fi antenna, they would search for retailers with vulnerable access points in their data systems.

They would steal confidential card data from these retailers. And then they would encode it on blanks, fake cards that could be used at ATMs. They would empty the accounts of every last dollar.

Like milking a cow until it's dry, as one federal prosecutor put it.

The crew stole card information from TJX, the parent company of Marshalls and T.J.Maxx, Dave & Buster's, 7-11, Barnes & Noble, JCPenney, and many others.

Along the way, Gonzalez connected with high-roller Internet thieves in Eastern Europe, including the Ukrainian cyber kingpin, Maksym Yastremskiy, who was then the world's biggest wholesaler of stolen cards.

Gonzalez would sell purloined card information to underworld dealers who resold the stolen data. He was paid staggering amounts of money through online currency exchanges, packages that would arrive with hundreds of thousands of dollars inside.

It was a high-stepping life for Gonzalez and his crew, and much of the money went up their noses.

Gonzalez threw himself a $75,000 birthday party in a New York hotel. Champagne flowed. Beautiful women prowled.

As prosecutors later described it, a table at the soirée served as a drug buffet. Partygoers could help themselves to a range of illicit substances served in the shape of initials. Cocaine, for example, was arranged on the table in the form of the letter C. Ecstasy was laid out in an E.

Apparently, Gonzalez and the rest of the gang weren't satisfied with the level of theft. Greedy for more money, they set their sights on the biggest prize: a credit card processor.

Heartland processes billions of card transactions a year. To the bad guys, we loomed as the ultimate target—*the mother lode*, as a prosecutor described us to the media, *the holy grail, the golden goose.*

As we would learn, the thieves had penetrated Heartland the day after Christmas in 2007. Using a Structured Query Language (SQL) attack, they began to study the topology of our corporate data system, searching for a way to get at the card information.

At first, they got only as far as the data systems in our corporate network. In June, they succeeded in jumping to our card processing system. While dates are difficult to pinpoint, it is believed the theft occurred for a handful of months, starting in mid-May of 2008.

Even before the first pieces of information were stolen, however, Gonzalez was behind bars in a Brooklyn jail.

The turning point in the case for the Feds came when investigators inspected computers used by the East European thieves. As investigators scrolled, they saw a mention of CumbaJohnny.

They knew that was the handle used by Gonzalez going back to his first days working for the government.

Inside the Secret Service, there were gasps:

He's one of ours.

The jig was up. On May 7, 2008, some 150 agents in SWAT formations fanned out in Miami. In Gonzalez' condo, they found computers and cash. They found the hacker himself in a room at the National Hotel in Miami Beach, with $22,000 in cash, two laptops and a Glock.

Police would recover more than $1 million that Gonzalez had wrapped in plastic bags and buried in a tube under a palm tree in his parents' back yard. They would seize his assets: a Miami condo, a BMW, a Tiffany diamond ring, three Rolex watches, the computer equipment and the handgun.

In U.S. District Court in Boston, lawyers for Gonzalez attributed his troubles to Asperger syndrome. They pointed to his behavior as an adolescent, noting that he was mesmerized by the computer. Psychologists who examined him refuted the Asperger claim as bogus.

As for spending an inordinate time on the computer, one observer noted dryly, the same could be said of half the students a short distance from the courthouse in the dorms at MIT.

Gonzalez also claimed during the trial that his only motive in committing the breaches was to satisfy a *technical curiosity*. But government logs revealed there was a little more to it than that.

He boasted about plans to make $15 million, buy a yacht and retire.

Gonzalez was sentenced to twenty years in prison for the cyber theft perpetrated against the many retailers, and he was sentenced to another twenty years for the attack on Heartland. The terms run concurrently.

Despite the growth in cybercrime, many businesses still do not always realize the devastating threats posed by a hacking attack.

As Doug Klotnia, of the cybercrime-auditing business, Trustwave, told an industry publication, the *Green Sheet*:

They still don't understand that a significant card breach is not a whole lot different than if their business burned down.

Credit card security breaches in corporations are even more common than people realize. While many high-profile breaches have been disclosed, there are many others you don't hear about. At plenty of companies, online attacks are treated, as a 2013 *New York Times* article put it, as *a dirty secret best kept from customers, shareholders and competitors.*

As the victim of a breach, I believed it was our ethical obligation to disclose it and help others understand what we learned. We saw it as our duty to work with others in the industry to safeguard against cyberthieves.

We even went to our competitors and gave them copies of the malware, the malicious software used in the breach, so they would know how to identify it in case it had been inserted into their own data centers by the bad guys. We told them everything we could about how Heartland had been penetrated, so they could prevent the same attack from happening to them.

Some people have asked: *Why would you help your competitors? After all, if one of them suffers a breach, doesn't that possibly mean more business for you guys at Heartland?*

That kind of thinking shows how cynical the corporate culture can become. We are perfectly happy to compete on the basis of delivering the best product and the best service. We don't want to succeed by having the crooks rob our competitors.

We helped develop an end-to-end encryption technology that scrambles card numbers into a code that cannot be detected by invaders—from the time the card is swiped until the processing of a purchase is entirely complete. We have shared much of this innovative technology with our competitors, and any company that wanted it.

Heartland also took the lead in forming an organization to share tools and information with other companies to combat cyber fraud. It's called the Payments Processing Information Sharing Council, and it works with law enforcement authorities to combat the hackers.

We were rewarded with kind words for our efforts. Richard S. Levick, a public relations expert, wrote in his book, *The Communicators*, that we took a potentially fatal incident and reacted in a way that actually strengthened our brand. We established our company as a thought leader committed to prevention, industry-wide solutions, honest communication, and putting customers and employees first.

Within a few weeks, Levick wrote, *news reports in the business media were spending as much, if not more, time on Heartland's successful response as on the life-threatening crisis itself.*

Businessweek published an article about what other companies could learn from Heartland. The magazine, *Computerworld*, ran a headline, *Heartland Commended for Breach Response*.

Jim Cramer, the host of *Mad Money*, meanwhile, pointed to Heartland's straightforward approach as something businesses should emulate.

But after the damage of the breach, we still had a long way to go to recover. Visa had taken us off their preferred list of processors, which we feared could be a virtual death sentence. We would win approval to get back on the list in April. It marked one of the fastest recoveries ever for a processor.

We lost only 2 percent of our customer base due to the breach, a whale of an accomplishment, given the circumstances. I believe that is owed to our salespeople going immediately to our customers and telling them everything.

It gave us a deep measure of credibility that can make all the difference with merchants, or anyone in the business world. It makes the difference in every sphere of life.

When you are willing to show people your warts, and not try to cover up things that are unpleasant, the customers are more likely to trust your word about everything else.

Being straightforward with employees and customers helped us recover in the market and make us even stronger. Our stock, which had plunged to $3.45, came back to nearly $15 per share by the fall of 2009, and before long would more than triple that number.

But at the time, we were scarcely out of the woods. The survival of the company remained very much in doubt. We had a huge—and uncertain—debt to settle.

When customers are defrauded, the card-issuing banks eat the cost, and make claims against the breach victim to recover the losses. It is the job of the processor, such as Heartland, to assure that card information remains secure and protected in transactions.

Our sponsor banks were Heartland Bank in St. Louis, and Key Bank in Cleveland. All parties needed to agree to a settlement.

The bottom line for Heartland was this: How much would Visa accept to settle the case? If they demanded a figure that was too high, as we believed they might, that would certainly put Heartland out of business.

The moment of truth would come in a meeting with Visa in November of 2009. Visa wields enormous power because it does more than 50 percent of all card business in the nation.

When I boarded a plane with Bob Baldwin to fly to the meeting in Cleveland, we knew our fate was in peril. Would we be returning to run the company? Or would Heartland die under the weight of an impossible legal proceeding?

When we met with Visa, it was Baldwin who took the lead. A forthright man, he got right down to brass tacks. We could pay 'X,' he explained, but that was as far as we could go.

The negotiator for Visa made her case for more money from Heartland. And then it was our turn once more.

It was a Kabuki dance.

The negotiations continued for an hour, two hours, three hours, and finally, nearly four hours, and then it was sealed.

You've got a deal, the woman from Visa said, sticking out her hand.

There were handshakes all around.

Afterwards, I turned to Baldwin and exclaimed: *We got through this! Can you believe it?*

It was also one of the proudest days of my life.

I knew, at last, that Heartland was going to survive.

3

PICKING YOUR POCKET

———————⋅✦⋅———————

Except for school texts and a large dictionary, I do not remember a book in our house growing up.

But my mother, Mary Frances Carr, was a teacher. She talked regularly to her children about the importance of the Golden Rule: *Put yourself in somebody else's shoes. If you want honesty, fairness and respect, treat others that way.*

I believed her message then, and still do today.

It might not be as sophisticated a concept in the financial world as interest rate swap derivatives, but I'd like to think it will be more enduring.

In the eyes of some in the business world, I guess that makes me a kind of a choirboy. So be it. Choirboys sometimes grow up to be street fighters.

If I had a chip on my shoulder, there were plenty of reasons for it.

In my early days, the president of the Bank of Illinois had reneged on a financial agreement. I had been the object of an attempted bribe at Parkland College. I had blown the whistle on a bank client who was playing games with the financing of his RVs and mobile homes. I had moved my family halfway across the country to take charge of a payment processing company, only to learn that it had more than a million dollars in hidden liabilities.

So I knew what it was like to be fleeced.

. . .

In the mid-1980s, when I entered the payment processing business, using a credit card could be a real hassle, for both the customer and the merchant.

If you wanted to use your card to buy, say, a microwave or a VCR (tech marvels in those days), the person behind the counter had to record a multi-copy, handwritten receipt. It meant searching through a booklet with small print to look up the card number, just to make sure your credit card was in good standing.

If the purchase exceeded a certain amount, maybe $25, a telephone call had to be made to the card processor to report the details of the transaction. And then there was the wait for approval.

When the store finally received the authorization code, it needed to be written down on the customer's credit slip. The slip was placed over the credit card, and then dragged through a mechanical imprinter, called a knuckle buster, to copy the number, the expiration date and the name embossed on the card.

At long last, the customer would then sign that paper slip, and a copy would serve as the receipt.

The people who were waiting in the growing line behind the customer, meanwhile, were likely to be scowling.

The transition to electronic processing came as a wonderful boon to efficiency. A swipe and a signature and you were out the door. It was a technology solution that enhanced revenue and attracted many into the business.

But the technological advance also provided an opening for a certain breed of business people, those who would peddle the electronic processing machines, known as terminals, as surefire money-saving machines.

Even when they weren't.

. . .

While every industry has honest and respectable people who are trying to do the right thing by their customers, there are also dishonest ones eager to take advantage of the uninformed.

Payment processing is tremendously complicated. While merchants rely on debit and credit transactions, most of them know little about what happens after the card is swiped. That makes them easy prey for con artists.

Each transaction involves several players: the card brands, such as Visa, MasterCard, American Express and Discover; the large banks that issue these cards; and the payment processor, such as Heartland, which provides the service and collects the fees. The processor distributes most of the collected fees to the card brands and to the banks. It keeps a smaller portion of the fees for providing its service.

In this complex system, most businesses have little idea about the flow of money and how the charges are apportioned.

Because the payments industry moves cash into and out of bank accounts by the billions every day, many are attracted to the industry. Unfortunately, not all of them have the best interests of their customers in mind. In fact, many see their customers as a pool of potential victims from which to extract unearned monies, simply because they know how to get away with it.

Many companies in our industry charge thousands of dollars for a machine that costs only a few hundred dollars. Other companies charge security fees, but provide no security service.

I have crossed paths with plenty of this brand of con artist. One was a guy out of Chicago who formed a company soon after serving time in prison for a conviction on bank fraud charges in Michigan.

Instead of selling an electronic terminal to a merchant, he would lease a machine for $49 or $69 or $89 or $159 a month, and then lock the merchant into a five-year noncancellable lease contract that automatically renewed. That added up to anywhere from $2,000 to $6,000 or more, a lot of money to pay for a $300 or $500 machine.

But the biggest problem for millions of business owners is that their bank deposits are deliberately shorted every month. They are essentially being robbed day by day. If an employer were to pocket one penny out of the net pay of an employee, they could be liable for criminal charges of theft. And there are many other ways to cheat customers. It happens regularly to many business people in America and there are no legal consequences for the pickpocket because of legal tricks well-known in the payments industry.

In some cases, even the salespeople don't realize they are swindling their customers because they don't understand the complexities of the business either. In other cases, they know exactly what they're doing.

It is perfectly legal, based on language buried somewhere in the pages of fine print of the agreement. The customers had simply put their trust in the salespeople. They were too busy running a hamburger joint, or an auto parts store, to spend hours poring over the long contract with small print.

Deception, outright lying and intimidation became so rampant in the payment processing business that Visa grew concerned about its own brand being tarnished. In 1988, the credit card giant came out with rules governing sales organizations that sold card transaction processing, which they designated as Independent Sales Organizations, or ISOs.

In that same year, a trade magazine article headlined, *Here Come the Tin Men*, described some of the prevailing misdeeds in the industry. I am proud to say that I served as a source for a lot of the material in the article. I named names because I loathed the crooks.

Some of my colleagues and I teamed up with a fellow ISO, Jay Hearst, a Harvard graduate, a guy with a stellar reputation in the business. In reaction to the new Visa rules, Jay had the idea to start a trade association to police the budding industry and to end the growing scams.

About a dozen of us gathered at the Hilton Hotel at O'Hare Airport in Chicago in 1988. That was the beginning of what would become a group called Bankcard Services Association, or BSA.

The felon sent two of his sales managers to that first meeting. There were introductions for each of the dozen or so people in attendance. When it was my turn, I explained that I had once been an officer of the Bank of Illinois. To hold such a position, I noted, you could not have a felony on your record.

I went on to say that since we handled millions of dollars of merchants' money, just like the banks do, it seemed right and logical that we should hold ourselves to the same standards.

If the organization was to allow felons to be members, I told the group that I would not be attending any further meetings.

We broke for lunch. The Chicago felon's sales guys never returned. The others stayed. Jay Hearst and the rest of us thought we had reason to be optimistic.

For the next eighteen to twenty-four months, we had several more meetings. But we were not making a lot of progress. At one of the meetings, several of us talked to the group about the need for ethical standards. Apparently my push for transparency and higher ethical standards in the business struck a raw nerve.

You know, Carr, your problem is that you don't have a business, one board trustee sputtered, *you have a religion!*

In 1989, the Bankcard Services Association officially organized. I was elected vice president. Jay was elected treasurer. The BSA was beginning to get some traction. We called a meeting in Denver in 1990, and it drew people from thirty or forty companies, a reflection of the growth in the payment processing industry.

Jay and I volunteered to serve on the ethics committee. As it turned out, the two of us *were* the ethics committee.

During the meeting, I made a motion that no convicted felons be allowed membership in the organization.

The measure was defeated.

I resigned and walked out.

Since those days, practices in our industry have gotten better in some ways, but worse in others. The trade organization, now called the Electronic Transactions Association, today has some 500 members in seven countries.

Unfortunately, many of the abuses endure. Felons are *still* allowed to be members of the organization. Some unscrupulous characters have simply become more sophisticated about the ways to take advantage of the unsuspecting business owners.

. . .

To the vast majority of consumers, credit and debit card fees are pretty much invisible. The cost doesn't show up as an item on the bill. Some people might even assume that banks pay the processing costs, given the profits on credit card interest that can soar into the 30 percent stratosphere.

But it's the merchant that pays for the service, and the smaller businesses on Main Street pay a vastly higher rate than the retail giants who own the big-box stores.

Every time a card is swiped, the merchant pays a fee, sometimes called a discount rate, which generally ranges anywhere from roughly 1.5 percent to 3.5 percent of the purchase, not counting monthly fees or transaction fees.

For many small businesses, these fees account for the third largest expense of operation, trailing only the cost of inventory and salaries for workers. In other words, the swipe fees often amount to a bigger cost than insurance, advertising and even rent.

Consider the struggles of an upstart entrepreneur. She must pay the rent, taxes and the salary of a sales clerk, as well as the product.

The salesperson walks into the store and promises that he can save her $1,000 a year if she switches the swiping process to him. To this aspiring entrepreneur, that's a lot of money.

All the merchant has to do, the salesperson promises, is lease his company's processing terminal for $59 a month. As time passes, the merchant realizes that the transaction fees have actually started to go way up.

The merchant wants to get out of this bind, but can't. According to the contract, she is stuck in the agreement for five years. She hadn't read the fine print, and doesn't think she can afford to hire a lawyer to look at the agreement.

When the business hits a lull in sales, the merchant is unable to pay the transaction costs. She can go to court, but will almost surely lose. And any unpaid debt will go on her credit report. That hurts anyone's chances of making it in business.

Not all payment processors treat their customers this way of course. But there are far too many predators out there.

The flim-flam artists of today don't look like the old street hustlers in black T-shirts, Rolex watches and gold bracelets. They wear expensive business suits. But they are even more treacherous.

4

YOU'RE COMING WITH ME

————————◆———————————

One of my most valuable employees returned to work for me in 1988. More accurately, I went to get her.

I drove my car with my wife, Jill, and my kids—Ryan, who was six, and Kelly, who was four—to Kalamazoo, Michigan, where my mother, Mary, had retired. She had moved into a subsidized apartment complex populated mostly by the elderly. It seemed to me that she had pretty much resigned herself at age sixty-four—a young sixty-four—to be packing it in. I think she felt she had no other options.

After all those years of standing on her feet as a waitress, my mother was suffering from cellulitis. I knew the condition was still painful for her, even though she had stopped waitressing years before to work in clerical roles at medical offices. But she was too young to be, as I saw it, giving up on life.

Besides, I needed her.

A partner and business manager of my struggling enterprise had pretty much disappeared, convinced that our business was headed for the rocks. I was left in the lurch.

I called my mother and told her I wanted her to run the company's tiny office. I was on my way to Michigan to pick her up and take her back to Florida with us.

She was less than enthusiastic.

I don't think I should do this, Bob, she said.

Well, I'm taking you anyway, I responded.

She would later tell me it was one of the best days of her life.

My mother had worked for me once before, in the late '70s, when my mainframe computer services business was transitioning into a personal computer software firm.

It was not long after she finally had left my dad.

She and my father had moved to Idaho just after I finished college, taking along my youngest siblings, Steve and Beth. As people who treat alcoholics would put it, my father was in search of a *geographical cure*. He had the view that if the world around him would just change, everything in his own life would get better.

The chance for a change of address came when his employer, Argonne National Laboratory, decided to expand its facilities in Idaho Falls. One day he came home and announced to my mom and siblings that they were going to pull up and move to Idaho.

No one dared object. That wasn't something you did with my dad.

The scenery changed, but little else. His drinking improved for a while, and then it worsened. His behavior grew even more dangerous. My mother, drawing on a well of fortitude nurtured in Al-Anon meetings, finally summoned the courage to leave him for good.

My mom was not a scholar and she was not erudite. She couldn't compose a profound academic thesis or craft a work of literature. But she had a brilliant mind that she used to help people.

She had a Ph.D. in a subject that could be titled, *Understanding Ordinary People.*

A lot of businesses could use more of her kind of wisdom. As Don Lassiter once put it: *Everything I ever needed to know about business, I learned on my mama's knee.*

Our car pulled up to her apartment complex. The kids hugged their grandma. Surprisingly, her belongings were already packed. Off we headed to Florida with our company's new office manager.

Mary Frances Evans was born on April 10, 1924, into a family of farm workers and day laborers in north central Missouri. Her father had been a railroad worker on the Rock Island Railroad. But there were long stretches without work.

Like so many other people of her generation, her childhood was shaped by the stinging privation of the Great Depression and the pangs of going without enough to eat.

The family drifted from place to place, looking for a job. Her father found work for a time in Dixon, Illinois. My mom enrolled in school and sat in the same classroom, and the same row, that had been occupied not so many years before by Ronald Reagan.

Dutch, as he had been known around town, would grow up to become president. He never won my mother's vote.

When it came to politics, my mother liked to say that she considered herself an Independent. Her voting record in presidential elections indicated otherwise: Harry S. Truman,

Adlai E. Stevenson (twice), John F. Kennedy, Lyndon B. Johnson, George McGovern, Jimmy Carter (twice), Hubert H. Humphrey, and Bill Clinton. All were Democrats, of course.

She was an Independent, all right, as long as the candidate didn't happen to be a *g$# damned Republican.*

From the time my mom was a little girl, until she became a young mother herself, Franklin Delano Roosevelt had led the nation. He remained a beloved figure throughout her life. In her view, he had saved the middle class and the poor with government programs.

It was FDR who once advised: *When you reach the end of your rope, tie a knot in it and hang on.*

That could have served as a motto for much of my mother's life. She was a woman who endured hardship, poverty and heartbreak, but never complained about her circumstances. As she saw it, there were always people who had it worse and people who had it better. She was satisfied to be *just about average.*

With the promise of work, she and her father left Dixon for Chicago. He found a job at International Harvester. With her mom and little sister still in Missouri, she lived with her dad in an apartment on Lavergne Avenue on the West Side of Chicago.

She was quiet, red-haired and fifteen years old. She played the baritone horn in the Austin High School band. In the same building lived a young man named Arthur Charles Carr, the son of the landlord. He was handsome, with jet black hair, a roaring motorcycle and a wild streak.

They married on December 20, 1941. He was twenty-two. She was seventeen. A little more than a year later, she gave birth to my brother, William Charles.

With my mother pregnant with me, my father went off to Amarillo, Texas, for training in the Army Air Corps. My mom temporarily moved in with her mother and sister in Missouri. I was born in November of 1945 in a hospital in Princeton, in Mercer County, Missouri. As it happened, I would later end up living in Princeton, in Mercer County, New Jersey.

After the war, my mother returned to Chicago to be with her husband. In April of 1947, she gave birth to her first daughter, Patricia Ann. Not yet twenty-three, she was the mother of three.

My father, a high school dropout, scrambled to make a living. He painted houses for a while, and then tried his hand at selling insurance. He later landed a job as a security guard at a federal research center, the Argonne National Laboratory, a nuclear reactor research center managed by the University of Chicago, in the far-flung corn and bean country south of the city.

My father was a city boy who idealized the good life in the country. My mother had moved so many times that she just wanted to settle down and have some stability. In 1948, they bought a two-bedroom house on an acre of land in the rural township of Homer, outside Lockport. The cost was $5,000 and the mortgage was $100 per month. The following year, my mom gave birth to Kathleen Mary. Steven Arthur was born two years later. Seven years after that came our baby sister, Elizabeth Jeanne.

It was a five-room house, and it was crowded. There were the six kids and my parents. And my grandmother, Lillian Owen Carr, lived there, too. She had a baby grand piano that took up almost half of the space we called the living room.

As we grew older, Bill and I shared a pull-out sofa bed in the living room. By that time, Pat, Kathleen, Steve and Beth shared beds upstairs in the walkway to Grandma's room. We were always right there in the middle of the action.

We saw plenty.

My mother worked the night shift at restaurants. She waited tables at the Big Run Golf Club in Lemont, the Candlelight in Plainfield, and the Blue Willow in Lockport. When she arrived home, she was exhausted.

She would collapse in a chair. Her feet soaked in a metal pan filled with warm water and Epsom salts. We kids would rub her feet.

One night she arrived home beaming with a sense of accomplishment. She had gotten her first $5 tip. It might have been the proudest I ever saw her.

Whenever she could, she brought home food and an occasional cream pie from the restaurant. My dad, meanwhile, came home every Friday with a couple of six-packs of Schlitz and a fifth of Jim Beam. He always had enough money for booze, and for some of his other indulgences, too. He couldn't afford to buy a dress for his daughters or a shirt or pair of pants for his sons.

My sisters, Pat and Kathleen, wore hand-me-downs from our mother's friends. You can imagine how fashionable it was for a teenage girl to wear the clothes of a middle-aged woman to high school in the 1960s.

When I started high school, I owned three hand-me-down shirts from my brother Bill, one pair of pants and one pair of shoes. But every week there was always money for booze, even at the end of the month, when we would often eat baked eggs or chicken necks and gizzards for dinner.

My father would sometimes bring along his buddies to drink, play cards and crack wise. Bogie, Swede and Frank were his pals. Like my dad, they really didn't like anyone of a different color and religion. When couples gathered, my mother would sit in the kitchen with the crowd and have a drink, eager to do anything that might pacify her husband.

My mother wasn't aware of it, at least as far as I knew, but my father had a habit of visiting houses of ill repute. I know because I once went along with him.

When I was 16, he decided it was time to drag me along for one of his many *man-to-man* lessons.

We drove to a neglected broken-glass precinct of Fairmont, a few blocks from Joliet on Highway 4A, and pulled up to a ramshackle bordello.

We walked inside and my dad reached for his wallet. The madam, or whatever you'd call the woman who ran the joint, looked at this father and son, and refused to do business.

To this day, I don't know if there just weren't any sex workers available at that moment, or if she wasn't about to get involved with a sixteen-year-old boy who looked even younger.

Every day, my father left the house at 7:30 a.m. and returned at 5:30 p.m., like clockwork. He hated his job. Even after he was promoted from his job of security guard to a position working inside the building, as an aide to the researchers at the lab, he saw his duties as nothing more than grunt work.

He despised bosses. According to my dad, people in management were villains. Business was evil and college-educated people were nothing more than pointy-headed jerks who thought they were better than everyone else.

One of the most important tenets of my career in business would be to create jobs that people didn't hate or, better yet, that they loved. I learned at an early age that unhappy workers bring their anger home with them.

. . .

My dad didn't give favorable reviews to his children either.

Who do you think you are? he would demand of us.

If we asked a question, he might respond, *Who are you with, the FBI?*

If there was ever an honest, meaningful conversation with my father, I do not remember it.

I remember one of my siblings describing his verbal assaults: *He could kill your soul.*

My mother spoke a different language. She told us that she loved each of her kids equally and unconditionally.

I once pressed her about this.

So you're telling me, I asked her, *that if I grow up to be a mass murderer who goes to prison, and my sister wins the Nobel Peace Prize, you're going to love us exactly the same?*

Exactly, she responded.

My parents had the bedroom downstairs and Grandma Carr had the bedroom upstairs. Grandma was not an especially warm or joyful person, even to her grandchildren, and it was no secret that she was discontented with the way her life had gone.

As a young woman, she had been an opera singer, an orchestra conductor and a teacher at the Sherwood Community Music School on Michigan Avenue in downtown Chicago. She had been a performer as well, recording operatic songs on vinyl 78s and singing in live performances broadcast on WLS radio in the 1920s.

She told my sister, Kathleen, that she had made it clear from the start that she wanted no part of marriage or motherhood, but preferred to live on her own as a professional in the music business.

The social mores of her day, however, didn't allow for such choices, and so she gave in to the traditional path.

She felt like she owed it to her father to give him a grandson. That was my dad, an only child.

Unhappy with her lot, my grandmother barely tried to conceal her resentments. Her life changed after my dad was born. And then she lost everything in the Depression.

Maybe that explains some things about my father.

At least that's how it seemed to my sister, Kathleen, who always tried to take a gentler view of him. She believed that he really wanted to be a good dad—he'd take us on day trips, take us swimming—but that he just didn't know how to show his children real love.

Kathleen thinks he was the product of an era where men were taught that showing tenderness was a weakness.

I take a less generous view.

I remember when my Grandmother Carr moved from our house to an apartment in town. My dad had pretty much evicted her. Still the arts maven, but virtually penniless, she was embarrassed that she needed to take government assistance.

When she lived in the subsidized apartment, I would walk from the high school to see her. She was lonely living by herself. It seemed that she had lost her will to live.

On one of these visits, she told me that when she died, she wanted to be buried next to her husband in the cemetery in Oak Park. I told her that she could count on me to make sure that happened. I told my dad about the promise.

When my parents moved to Idaho, they took Grandma Carr with them. As she grew gravely ill, I remembered my vow to make certain she would be buried in Oak Park. I flew to the hospital in Idaho to visit her before she died, and to make arrangements to have her body transported back to Illinois.

She died as I flew back to Illinois. When I called my father and reminded him I had made the burial plans, he told me he would be the one making the decision.

I had her body cremated.

He did not even save the ashes.

Long before, I had decided to study and learn from my dad's life and become just the opposite of him—in the way he lived and treated others and himself. Most of all I wanted to have a life that I could look back on and be proud of. My mother ultimately left my father after unspeakable events. He soon married a woman named Pat, who divorced him after several of his drunk-driving convictions.

She once dumped his clothes in the yard outside of her house. He responded by breaking all of the windows in the place.

In divorce court, when things didn't go his way, my dad grew so furious that he threatened to kill the judge.

In one of his trials, a judge gave my father a choice: counseling or jail.

My dad chose jail.

After a brief taste of the austerity of incarceration, my dad decided he would be willing to give rehab a try after all.

But three days into the program, the counselors kicked him out of the place.

It takes a lot, I am told, to be kicked out of a rehab program.

When my father retired from Argonne at age sixty-two, he was given the choice between a monthly pension and a lump sum payment.

He took the pile of cash.

When he collected the money, he drove straight to Jackpot, Nevada, and gambled away every penny of it.

Homeless and without a job or a friend or a dollar to his name, he began a campaign to beg from anyone he had ever known. Some of us tried to help him.

My dad had grown up on the West Side of Chicago near Oak Park. Two famous men had risen from Oak Park when my father was a young man—Frank Lloyd Wright and Ernest Hemingway.

In my childhood, I listened to my dad talk many times about the famous author and the way he ended his life, by putting a gun in his mouth and pulling the trigger.

One day in 1981, I had finished a business meeting in Oklahoma when I picked up a ringing phone. It was my mother. She had called to tell me that my father had shot and killed himself.

My mother explained that she was arranging a proper memorial service for her ex-husband in Lockport, in the basement of the First Congregational Church.

She told me she expected me to be there.

I just can't do it, Mom, I told her from Oklahoma. *I have work to do. Can't we do it later?*

You're coming, she told me, *and you're coming now.*

And so I did.

Jill and I drove the seventeen hours to Lockport. We gathered in the church across from Corwin's, where he had given me his man-to-man talk.

When my mother came to work and live with us in Florida, she set up shop in a spare bedroom of our ranch-style three-bedroom house.

Jill paid the bills. My mother handled the calls from customers. It was a job she loved. And everyone seemed to love her.

I can remember hearing her talk on the telephone with customers in distant area codes, ostensibly about some issue relating to payment processing. You would have thought she was chatting with old friends and neighbors.

Is school going all right for your daughter? How did the visit to the relatives go? I'll say a prayer that your mom feels better.

She brought to work a sense of values that had always guided her actions. When we were kids, my mother made it clear that honesty, compassion and fairness were tantamount. All people were equal and deserved to be treated with respect, no matter their position.

When I was a kid, I had come to learn that, for a time, we were the only family we knew who had to shovel coal to heat the house.

Are we poor? I asked her.

She thought for a moment.

Some people have more than we do, she explained, *and plenty of people have it a lot harder. We are about average.*

It was a perspective that gave her a lens for just about everything in life. We were no better than others and others were no better than us.

My mother understood some things about business that plenty of brilliant MBAs never grasp.

Customers are people. They have feelings and fears and hopes that reach far beyond the business deal of the day. She cared about them, even if she had never seen them in person.

A customer could call the office with a complaint, so irate you could hear the screaming on the phone. After talking with my mother for a few minutes, the caller would grow calm and reassured, knowing that someone had listened. She was going to make darned sure that everything got fixed.

If a customer had a problem, she genuinely worried about it. It wasn't just a business matter. She empathized with the real human being on the other end of the line. These were people who were experiencing a struggle. They needed help.

As a woman who grew up without means and then raised
a family without much, she rooted for underdogs and people
at the margins. She saw most people as trying to do their best.
Things just hadn't worked out for them.

She prized honesty. The misfortunes of life might take away
all of your possessions, as she liked to say, but no one could ever
rob you of your integrity. The only person who could cause you
to lose your self-respect, she explained, was you. She said that
people who cheat others can't have much self-respect.

She lived what she taught, and people in the company noticed.

Employees learn what they see, much more than what they
hear. She would never have taken credit for it, but my mom
played a major role in helping to shape the 'corporate culture' at
our company.

After Jill and I and our kids moved to Princeton in 1992,
my mother lived in our ranch house in Florida. And with my
frequent flyer miles, she finally got a chance to travel the world.

She took a cruise over the seas of Alaska. She took a tour of
Europe and returned the following year to see the Passion Play
at Oberammergau in Germany. She sailed the Caribbean twice.
She visited Hawaii and the Bahamas. She toured Chichen Itza
in Mexico. Most meaningful to her, she was honored by her
grandchildren at a family gathering in Montreal.

She said she considered herself the luckiest person in
the world.

I was preparing for a Saturday trip to Dallas when the
telephone rang. My mother was calling to tell me that she was in
the hospital. She stressed that it was no big deal. There was this

little heart incident, she explained, but she was absolutely fine. Not to worry. Go ahead with the trip to Texas.

She sounded like her normal happy self. But she seemed tired. I asked her to pass the phone to the nurse.

You heard my mom, I said to the nurse. *What should I do?*

With a tone of urgency, the nurse told me: *Your mother has had a heart attack.*

I called my brothers and sisters, and most of us headed immediately to the hospital in Florida.

When I arrived, it was late at night and my sister, Kathleen, who is a nurse, was at my mom's bedside. My mother said she was going to be fine.

She did complain of a bad headache. And she handed me the keys to her car.

She died the next morning. She had suffered a brain aneurysm. It was Mother's Day of 1993. She was sixty-nine years old.

It was the worst day of my life.

It wasn't time for her to die. I did not have the chance to tell her goodbye. If ever I had a tragedy in my life, this was it.

Her funeral was held at the Brandon Christian Church in Florida, where she had volunteered in the kitchen and helped with the youth programs.

I gave the eulogy. It was nine pages long. Many of the flowers in the church had come from people who had grown to cherish their relationship with my mother, but had never met her in person. They had been comforted by her words on the telephone.

After all she had been through, my mother never sought to settle scores or nurse grievances. Just weeks before her death, she had sat down and wrote a letter to my dad.

I must say goodbye now, it began. *I pray to God in heaven that you are there when he takes me to be with Him.*

It was signed: *My love always and in all ways, Mary.*

According to her wishes, she was buried alongside my father's ashes near our Illinois home in Homer Township.

5

I COULDN'T BELIEVE WHAT I SAW

———————◆◆———————

When I walked into our Heartland call center in Indiana, a renovated bowling alley, it was supposed to be a celebratory grand opening, a moment of triumph for our company.

I was appalled. I couldn't believe what I was seeing.

In terms of growing and making a profit, our company was soaring. But when it came to the way we were treating some of our employees, we had taken a serious wrong turn.

With Heartland growing so rapidly, we were struggling to keep pace hiring enough new employees to answer calls from our clients.

The callers were typically merchants who had a problem—maybe a terminal had gone down—and our people were on the line to figure out a way to fix it, and fix it quickly.

For the call center, we had rented some space in the Youngstown Shopping Center in Jeffersonville, Indiana, just across the Ohio River from Louisville, Kentucky. The strip mall had several other tenants, including a Sherwin Williams paint store. Whenever a space would become available, we would snap it up to make room for our burgeoning work force. We eventually took over the adjacent bowling alley.

The directors of my board insisted that I start to do more delegating. It was hard to argue against that idea. The company was growing too large for me to try to manage so much. I needed help. So I hired a new president to manage some aspects of operations, including the demands of our call center.

He promised me that things would be running smoothly. He hired a manager, a real pro, he said, a guy with experience operating a big call center in the Philippines for our largest competitor, First Data.

When I checked on the progress, my president reported cheerfully that things were going swimmingly.

I had reason to believe otherwise.

We were losing about one-third of our new hires even before they had completed training. Another one-third were quitting before completing their first year at the company.

I scheduled a trip to see the remodeled bowling alley. My president and his call center czar looked forward to my visit. They were very pleased with the efficient, highly disciplined operation they had created. They were certain that I would be delighted, too.

I was nauseated.

When I walked into the place, I saw all of these little cubicles, fitted together tightly, almost as far as the eye could see. People were working in what resembled tiny cages.

I looked up to the ceiling and saw rows of offices with smoked glass. The people inside them could see out. But the workers below couldn't see in.

It amounted to surveillance, and it was demeaning.

Behind the glass in these vaunted offices sat the supervisors, peering down on the minions, who were working their tails off on the telephones and, no doubt, worrying about being judged by their faceless taskmasters.

It shamed me. It was a perversion of what Heartland stood for.

Those workers on the phones, after all, were standing on the shoulders of Mary Frances Carr.

I was damned if any call center dictator was going to make a mockery of my mother's guiding philosophy: *No one is superior—and no one is inferior—to a fellow human being.* I had heard those words when I was a little kid. Although she had now been gone for a handful of years, her words still echoed.

I approached the president and the call center manager and asked some questions.

Why were the work spaces so small and narrow? Why were the supervisors spying behind smoked glass? And why were they looking *down* on our fellow employees?

They looked at me like I was some kind of naive country boy, and responded in a condescending tone.

Look, we know what we're doing...and anyway...what experience do YOU have in running a large call center?

I went off searching for another opinion. I asked for a perspective from one of the highest ranking executives in the company. He told me that the president and the call center manager were right. He seemed to suggest I was being soft.

Face it. These people are lucky just to have jobs.

It made me question myself. What did I really know? I had never worked in an organization of even half this size before. We had some very smart people telling me I was wrong. Maybe I *was* the problem.

I hired a management consultant in Philadelphia to do some research and give me some advice. I needed to get to the root of this dissension. I wanted her to get the views of half a dozen or so executives at Heartland and then make a recommendation to me about a course of action.

It didn't take long for the consultant to deliver her findings. Sitting in my office, she rested her chin in her hand and looked at me inquisitively.

Bob, she asked, *why is it that you don't feel you have the right to fire people who don't share your values?*

She was right. The call center workers shared my values, not the top brass.

The next day, I dismissed the president.

And the expert who designed the glass prison fortress at the call center? He would be gone, too.

He now works for a competitor.

After the personnel changes, I returned to the Jeffersonville center and arranged for an all-hands meeting. We rented a ballroom for a meeting with about 250 employees at the Holiday Inn in nearby Clarksville, Indiana.

Standing before my colleagues, I delivered an apology.

We are changing the model here, I said. *We are going to stop hiring people and treating them like we don't really like them.*

I made it plain that I considered their jobs vital to the success of the company. They were doing important work that truly mattered in the lives of people. When a customer has trouble, our call center workers are coming to the rescue, making it possible for our clients to pay bills, support their kids, sleep peacefully. They were solving problems and changing lives for the better.

That is why, I reminded them, that we needed to have our very best people taking phone calls.

And that's why we would be increasing starting wages by 50 percent—as soon as we could meet our goals in improving efficiency and productivity. About six months later, pay for starting employees at the center went from $10 to $15, more than double the minimum wage at the time.

For a big share of the year, I returned to Jeffersonville for follow-up meetings with our call center team. I shared with the employees our plans to build a beautiful new service center, a place that would stand for the way we believe workers should be treated.

Fixing our problem required no management wizardry or consultancy brilliance. It was simply a matter of treating other people with the respect and decency they deserve.

I am happy to report that the bowling alley days are long gone. Our service center employees now come to work at a stately brick facility that looks like a sparkling new corporate campus. At 215,000 square feet, it dwarfs the size of most corporate headquarters, including our own.

The $85 million complex sits on nearly forty acres of rolling prairie and forested land. Employees look through huge windows that let the sun shine through. The land is dotted with oaks, maples, pine and sycamores. From inside the service center, you can still see the silo and barn on the old dairy farm where the McCormick boys grew up years ago, as some of our employees with local roots can tell you. And from certain parts of our service center, you can see the skyline of Louisville. The center sits proudly on the road circling the center, Heartland Way.

On brick patios in the fresh air, colleagues at the call center fix themselves meals at gas grills. Our cafeteria, *Food for Thought*, provides plenty of healthy fare. Our library stocks publications that range from *Rolling Stone* magazines to the poetry of Kahlil Gibran.

We have a quiet room on the first and second floors, where employees who need a rest can retreat and restore. Research shows that employees often go home with a headache, but would probably remain at work if they just had a chance to lie down, close their eyes and rest for thirty minutes or so.

Our fitness center, managed by my daughter, Corrie Nichols, is open every minute of the year. It has a full complement of treadmills and barbells. It is surrounded by a running track that measures one-twentieth of a mile. A personal trainer works Mondays through Fridays, and the fitness center staffs a massage therapist, too.

Our new office layout has no tiny cubicles or spying glass offices of the old days. We don't have cubicles. We don't even have offices. The desks are open and curved in a way designed to be ergonomically friendly. Teammates can turn around and speak with one another.

The people in charge work at desks, too, among everyone else. Marty Moretti, the manager of the whole operation, doesn't have an office; neither does Jeff Nichols, the second-in-charge, who happens to be my son-in-law.

People are trusted to do a good job, without pestering. As one worker put it:

When you're on the phone talking with your mother, and she's telling you that she needs a ride to the doctor, you don't have to worry anymore about a boss tapping you on the shoulder.

Our rate of turnover, meanwhile, has fallen to very low levels.

I see it as Herb Kelleher of Southwest Airlines sees it. A business has three sets of constituents: the employees, the customers and the shareholders. A lot of businesses like to say that the customers are the most important part of the equation. That's not my view. I believe the employees are even more important.

If you have happy employees, they will take good care of the customers. Satisfied customers, in turn, translate to healthier corporate profits. That, naturally, will make the shareholders smile.

6

A CAPITALIST'S CRITIQUE OF CAPITALISM

It probably wasn't what the crowd expected to hear from the chief executive of a Fortune 1000 company.

I was a capitalist talking about capitalism as it is practiced today. And I was not exactly a cheerleader.

I had been invited to participate in a panel at Princeton University on global sustainability. It was essentially a discussion about how to make the world a better place, from climate and the arts, to government and business. The audience included faculty and staff, as well as others who live in the area. I was there to represent the perspective of someone from the world of commerce.

I decided to turn the tables and asked the people in the crowd some questions.

How many of you are invested in the stock market?

Some hands went up, but not all.

Well, how many of you have a 401(k)?

Now just about everyone raised a hand. So they agreed that they were all investors in the market.

I asked them to talk about their investment goals.

The consensus: Everyone wanted to make as much money as possible. They wanted the stocks in their portfolios to zoom to the sky.

How many of you care how the companies earn their money? I asked. *Or is the size of the return all that matters?*

These were smart, well-intentioned people, and I have no reason to believe that any of them would ever overtly condone bad corporate behavior or unethical practices. But that wasn't the point.

None of them mentioned taking any steps to look into the practices of companies and learn how they treat their employees or their consumers.

I told them that was a key problem with capitalism.

People were more than a little surprised. It wasn't what they had expected to hear from me. But that's how I see it.

If profit is your only goal as a stockholder, you're essentially telling the board of directors and the management that you don't care what they do to turn a profit.

You're in effect telling them: Spare me details of the sausage-making, so to speak, the unseemly transactions that exist behind the scenes in politics or business. Just show me the money.

Not everyone turns a blind eye, of course. In the days of Apartheid rule, many people refused to invest in South African businesses. Some people today won't invest in tobacco companies, of course. That's an easy target.

When it comes to the vast majority of companies, however, people on the outside have very little knowledge, if any, about the conditions facing employees. For that matter, the average investor in mutual funds probably couldn't name many of the companies in their portfolio.

The CEO answers to a board of directors, and the board is usually pressing hard for growing profits, and this is to be expected. The board will generally favor whatever action it takes to meet that goal, as long as it stays within the law. For many CEOs and management teams, however, even staying within the law is made into a gray area. Before Heartland was founded, I attended one board meeting where the vice chairman said flatly, *I don't care if it is black and white; figure out a way to make it gray.*

Management answers to the board who answers to the stockholder. If more people looked into the behavior of the companies they're helping to bankroll, and called them out on unfair practices, it would make a difference. Boards pay attention when investors start asking questions. When investors aren't paying attention, management is often given a pass to do bad stuff.

In 2011, as part of an effort to address abuses in the payments market, Congress passed a measure known as the Durbin Amendment to the Dodd-Frank banking reform bill. The Durbin Amendment lowered debit card fees being paid by merchants to the big banks. The spirit of the law clearly intended that payment processors, who collect those fees, would pass on the savings to their merchant-clients just as they pass on all price increases from the card networks.

But that didn't happen in most cases. Instead, many of the processors changed their billing statements, which were already confusing, to obscure the newly discounted rates. Virtually all of the processors put a lot of the savings intended for merchants into their own pockets.

We were the *only* major company in the industry to return every penny to every customer, more than $750 million so far. To this day, some people at Heartland lament that we didn't do the same thing as our rivals. It would have fattened our profits without a lick of work and virtually nobody would even know it.

Everybody else is doing it? Why not us?

Because it would have been ethically wrong, even if it wasn't technically against the law. That's why.

It is little surprise that ordinary people have lost so much respect for big business, especially in matters of finance. Consider the way so many banks take advantage of customers who experience an overdraft.

These checking account fees have become a cash cow—make that an entire herd of cash cows! U.S. banks in 2013 collected about $32 billion in overdraft fees—almost $100 for every man, woman and child in the country. Each charge typically exceeds $30, even if it's for a transaction that is much lower.

While the fees average $34, a majority of the overdrafts involve transactions of $24 or less, according to federal regulators, and are paid back within three days.

This is egregious gouging. Richard Cordray, the director of the Consumer Financial Protection Bureau, put it this way:

If a consumer were to get a loan on those terms, that would equate to an annual percentage rate of over 17,000 percent.

A rate of 17,000 percent!!!

I would like to sit on a panel with someone from the banking industry and ask them to defend the moral basis for imposing such unfair rates—charges which fall heaviest, of course, on uninformed paycheck-to-paycheck people who are most vulnerable to such rip-offs.

The financial institutions will tell you that the consumer has agreed to such arrangements. Indeed, federal regulators in 2010 implemented a requirement that customers must choose, or opt-in, to a stipulation that covers overdrafts. These exorbitant fees are marketed as overdraft *protection*. A more proper description would be overdraft *rip-offs*. It's buried somewhere in all of those pages of fine print. It is scarcely surprising that a Pew study found that 52 percent of those being charged do not recall opting in for such costly coverage. They were enticed by the promise that their checks would not be returned, but didn't understand that the cost for this *service* would be so high.

It gets worse. A survey by the *Wall Street Journal* in 2014 found that 16 percent of financial institutions process checking account transactions on a high to low basis to maximize the fees. In other words, the banks deduct the day's largest withdrawal before they deduct the smaller ones, depleting the account balance faster. That means more checks or debit transactions will bounce. And since the fees themselves draw down the balance, yet more transactions will be snagged for costly fees.

These are the kinds of techniques that some fancy business schools have taught future bankers in the quest to fatten profits. It's working. Federal regulators estimate that overdraft fees account for more than 60 percent of the margin collected by banks on checking and debit accounts. So much for *free* checking!

The casters of the first stone will remind us that people can avoid such problems by avoiding overdrafts. That is so. For people fortunate enough that their pockets have always been full enough to pay the bills, good for them. Plenty of the rest of us, however, know the sinking feeling of being in the negative.

The bank branch managers on Main Street, who often have to face neighbors who are understandably upset about the outrageous charges, have little room to maneuver. If they try to reverse these fees, the money often comes out of their pockets.

I have a question for some of the workers at those financial institutions: How well do you sleep at night when you know your employer is taking advantage of the most vulnerable like this? I know the moral hazard argument—letting people get away with overdrafts will stimulate bad behavior. But there are very effective ways in place to combat this problem—at a cost much less than $32 billion every year—costs assessed to the very people in our society who are least able to afford them.

. . .

In the earlier days of our company, when I controlled a majority of the stock, I decided to give away about one-third of my shares. As I saw it, giving away that portion of my ownership would not materially change my life, but it would make a big difference to my colleagues at Heartland. And it made me feel good about sharing the wealth with those who helped create it.

I distributed the shares to executives and other top-level people, as well as to hourly workers who had been with the company for more than two years. That won a lot of appreciation in the ranks, and it gave our workers even more incentive to make the company a success.

The *Wall Street Journal* wrote a story about my philosophy under a headline, *Share the Wealth.*

I just happen to believe that if you're going to work your butt off to help make me wealthy, you deserve some of the riches, too.

After the breach, when I lost my fortune, the board designed a compensation package for me with stock options and incentives tied to the performance of the company. It has been a very good run. Since the harrowing events of 2009, the value of Heartland has grown from a low of $150 million after the breach to nearly $2 billion.

My own financial circumstances, as a result of the company's success, have taken a most fortunate turn. I won't likely ever be worth over $300 million, as I once had been, but I have become very prosperous, indeed. I will be able to send a lot more deserving kids through college.

You *can* find businesses that pay well, respect workers *and* achieve bottom-line success.

Zeynep Ton, an MIT professor, has argued that treating employees as partners is a smart long-term business strategy. In her book, *The Good Jobs Strategy*, she cites Costco as an example of a successful company that pays better than average wages and wins in the marketplace.

But too often, she has said, companies tend to see employees as little more than *an interchangeable part*. And she noted, *Workers feel that.*

In our company, we do not tolerate behavior that is belittling or demeaning to another human being. It doesn't matter if it's a boss reprimanding an employee. There is no excuse. In a memo I once delivered to the company: *If you feel you need to blow off steam, go do it somewhere else.*

Treated with support and respect, employees will have the back of a business leader.

When I sent a note of thanks to Rick Walters for working so hard to solve IT operational issues, his reply left me deeply humbled and grateful. And he offered a powerful insight:

Over the last couple of decades, there has been a shift in the attitude most people have about their employers, Rick wrote. *It was said that if you asked an American what they did for a living, the response would be, 'I'm a programmer,' or 'I'm an engineer.' If you asked a Japanese person that question, you would get, 'I work for Sony,' or 'I work for Toyota.'*

The employer-employee relationship has changed quite a bit in this country. I am not convinced it's a change for the better. You have made me proud to say, 'I work for Heartland Payment Systems.'

• • •

In general, business leaders don't like to make waves. Like everybody else, executives like to be popular among their peers. They want to be able to go to a conference and relax over a drink without worrying about someone looking cross-eyed at them because they spoke an unpleasant truth. And some certainly don't want to invite scrutiny to their own practices.

But it's worth considering the power for change that lies with an outspoken leader.

What if a credible leader in the mortgage industry, before the housing bubble burst, had stood up and said: *Hey, these are criminal acts and we've got to put a stop to it!*

Maybe it would have made a difference.

The economic meltdown still casts a long shadow. Many of those who were lured into lying about their incomes lost their homes. Plenty of them will likely never be able to buy a house again.

And exactly how many Wall Street villains went to jail?
Zero.

David Uhl, a senior vice president of consulting services for
Aubrey Daniels International, wrote in the *American Banker* in
2014 about how bottom-line myopia can cause an institution to
become vulnerable to unethical behavior.

*The issue is not that people working in banks are inherently
duplicitous,* he wrote. *It's that they are under a great deal of pressure
from top management, often operating under the perception that their
jobs are on the line. Meanwhile, employees who would like to speak
up and disagree with questionable behavior are afraid they will be
punished if they do so.*

As Uhl underscored, problems arise when businesses
emphasize *results* rather than *behavior. A loan officer's incentive
pay,* he noted, *is often driven by sales and profit goals, without any
accountability for risk management.*

Bank management should...hold back from celebrating good results,
he advised, *until they know the behaviors that produced them.*

It naturally galls people that the powerful in business don't
seem to be playing by the same rules as everyone else. And it
tarnishes the vocation of business, stoking the skepticism of
people like my mom, and turning bright young people away
from a career in commerce where they are needed very badly.

The bad guys in business don't always get away with it, of
course. Ask the imprisoned Bernie Madoff. Or take a look at
the Enron *geniuses*, who once strutted so proudly and lavished
themselves like there was no tomorrow. It's worth remembering
that Charles Ponzi, the genius of the pyramid scheme, ended up
going to prison and then died in poverty in a charity hospital in
Brazil in 1949.

But a century after Woodrow Wilson created the Federal Trade Commission in 1914, we have more deceptive practices than ever.

As a kid, I got an earful about the sins of business from my parents. My mother was not happy when I decided to become an entrepreneur in my mid-twenties.

Why do you think you're better than the rest of us? she asked.

I didn't believe that, of course, but she had always felt like the moneyed classes had looked down their noses at people like her.

She believed the successes of business people would bite them in the end. She saw an inverse relationship between money and happiness.

Just look at Elizabeth Taylor. So much glamour, fame and fortune. And it's one divorce after another!

My mother, for her part, never had much experience with money, at least not with any real disposable income.

But she *was* an entrepreneur. As a waitress, she worked for tips. The better she served her customers, at least in theory, the more money she would earn.

I am proud to be an entrepreneur. Business can be a very honorable pursuit. It can change lives for the better.

It is heartening to look at the practice of providing microloans, for instance, which help establish start-ups in developing countries. These are enterprises vital to economic growth in desperately poor communities around the world. And these businesses are often run by women who could not otherwise obtain conventional financing.

Concepts like microloans blossomed at college campuses. Bright students saw that business could be a force for good. It is my hope that growing numbers of idealistic young people, the sort of kids who want to promote social justice and save our world, will join the ranks of entrepreneurs.

We need them.

7

MAKING MORE THAN THE BOSS

———————◆◇◆———————

While chief executives like to see employees do well, it often has its limits.

I'll be damned if anyone is going to make more money than me! I have all of the pressure and get all of the blame if something goes wrong. Why shouldn't I always earn the most?

I was absolutely thrilled when fourteen Heartland employees, all of them sales pros, earned higher compensation one year than did Robert O. Carr, the CEO. The truth is, the CEO isn't *always* the one creating the most value.

When I started the company, I set a goal to build a business so healthy and prosperous that more than one hundred employees would become millionaires. We've surpassed that goal.

In the years before we went public, I was confident that the value of our stock would soar. We created a program that encouraged our people to set aside part of their monthly earnings—up to $2,500 a month—to be deposited in bank accounts to exercise stock options later.

On the day we went public, employees who set aside money for the stock options saw an eightfold increase in the value of their savings. Their hard work and foresight made many of them wealthy. They deserved it. Our initial public offering created more than seventy millionaires. Most were in the management team and the sales organization. But people in many other departments, too, became newly minted millionaires. It stands as one of the great stories in American business.

People who work in sales don't always get the respect they deserve. Selling is hard work. It requires the creativity to figure out ways to reach potential clients, the psychological and physical stamina to *put yourself out there,* and the emotional resilience to withstand rejection.

It takes a special breed to work as a salesperson or on a purely commission basis. These are risk-taking entrepreneurs. They understand both the downside and the upside.

Plenty of the best salespeople have overcome adversity in their careers and personal lives. Maybe they've tried a line of work and failed. Maybe they simply didn't fit into somebody else's system. Some of them didn't like having someone constantly looking over their shoulders. Others are simply natural entrepreneurs who love to be in control of their lives.

Maybe that's why I like these people so much. I can relate to them.

I believed the salespeople who were building the portfolio of the company deserved a piece of the action. They should have an ownership stake in the part of the business that would not exist without them.

The idea was viewed as radical and downright crazy by many in the sales management world. We devised a compensation plan that allowed our salespeople to build equity in their portfolio, based on their residuals, or commissions. If they chose to do so under the guidelines, they could sell the value of their equity back to the company—at a sum that is thirty times the monthly residual earnings.

In other words, a vested sales professional earning $6,000 a month in residual commissions can exchange those payments for a lump sum of $180,000.

Rivals in the industry called us fools. They predicted that we would go broke.

To the contrary, this sharing of the ownership stake became a powerful engine for growth for Heartland. For our salespeople, it means the chance to amass a sizable chunk of money.

It has given some people the opportunity to sell portions of their portfolio and make the down payment for a house or pay for a child's tuition. One of our people said it allowed her to step away from work for a while and care for her children in the aftermath of a difficult divorce.

Others have used the money to leave their jobs and start a new career of their dreams. We hate to lose someone that way, but our people are free to live the lives they want to live. Fortunately, the vast majority like Heartland's brand of freedom and never want to leave.

Earnings for our sales professionals are uncapped. Unlike other companies, we don't put a limit on earnings or change the commission plan to make it more difficult to earn wealth.

Bob Donnelly, an executive director at Heartland, remembers working for another company and making a huge sale. He didn't receive his just share, however, simply because *that's just too much money* to pay as a commission.

There is no concept of *too much money* for an employee at Heartland. If they earned it, they're going to receive it. And it doesn't matter if it amounts to more than the paycheck for the CEO.

I have never subscribed to the notion that people needed to fit a certain mold to be a success in life or in business.

When Blaine Burn was growing up near Tulsa, Oklahoma, his counselor at Catoosa High School suggested that he wasn't cut out for college. Blaine was advised to consider a trade. For some reason, they thought he would make a fine welder.

Blaine never learned to weld. And he still doesn't have a college degree. But he has the smarts, personality and tenacity that led to a brilliant future in sales. At Heartland, he became a multimillionaire.

When a salesperson makes a killing and receives a big paycheck, some companies get uncomfortable. They should be grateful.

Back in the early days, Jim Lefler, a sales champ, won a trip with his wife anywhere in the world for being our top sales producer. He called to thank me.

I told him he had it exactly backwards. I owed him a debt of gratitude.

Do you realize, I asked him, *that you made it possible for us to meet payroll last month?*

When a company succeeds, the leaders are revered as geniuses, and when it falls short, the leaders are scorned as incompetents.

It is the employees, to a far greater degree than is recognized, who have the power to make or break a business.

When Lefler joined our team, he was broke.

Or, as he puts it, he and his wife, Jacqui, were *worse than broke*.

He had no money, and he owed plenty. At age forty-five, with four young children, he knew that awake-at-night feeling of financial panic.

Jim had spent twenty-five years in a family clothing business in his native Arkansas. The business had thrived in his father's day. But times had changed. Customers were drifting to the big-box stores.

Desperate to find a path to economic survival, Jim heard about this new company named Heartland. He got on a plane in March of 1998 and flew to a hotel in Dallas, where Don Lassiter and I had convened a training session for people interested in joining our business.

Within a year, Jim was *blowing it up*, as he colorfully puts it, achieving great success in landing new business.

When we opened the new service center near Louisville, I asked Jim to move to Kentucky to lead our sales efforts in the state. By this time, he was making enough money to pay down a lot of his debt, but he still didn't have much in the way of any savings for a down payment. He and Jacqui hadn't owned a home in five or six years.

They saw a place they loved in the horse country near Lexington, but couldn't qualify for financing.

I co-signed the loan, and they were able to move into their dream home.

Jim was astonished that I would back his mortgage. It came down to trust. The way I saw it, I was investing in someone I respected, someone whose hard work had helped make our company a success. And besides all of that, it made me feel good to be able to help someone.

Eventually, Jacqui would become a great employee for Heartland, too. So it's fair to say that the company made out great on the whole deal. It was worth every penny of my investment.

In business, if everything boils down to *only* profits, people learn pretty quickly that you don't care much about them as a human being. They grow a little wary. They keep an emotional distance.

That can be very isolating for a business leader. People start telling you only what they think you *want* to hear. Even worse, they become afraid to tell you what you *need* to hear.

I only know what has worked for us. As I see it, if you're leading a business, you need to let people know that you truly care about them. While talk of bad behavior by a CEO spreads fast, word of good deeds gets around pretty quickly, too.

For a time, Jim traveled around the country and talked to our salespeople about the Heartland philosophy. It was about more than business. It was also about reaching your potential as a human being, finding meaning as a person, and not just as a successful worker and a high earner.

You don't want to be one-dimensional.

As Jim put it, *A wheel can't roll if it's flat on one side.*

Like a lot of our successful sales pros, Jim drew on talents that might not seem to have much to do with credit card transactions. As a young man, he had been an aspiring musician. He remembered as a kid watching Ed Sullivan introduce the Beatles and seeing the crowd go berserk. He saw the pretty girls practically faint at the site of the Fab Four.

I watched all that, he recalled, *and I thought, 'That's what I want to do!'*

After finishing college in Arkansas in the '70s, he moved to Nashville, where he played bass for a band owned by Tanya Tucker, the country music star. They played at state fairs around the country, and were able to draw some pretty big crowds to some pretty remote places. Jim played the rodeo in the Nebraska Sandhills country of Valentine three times.

He once found himself sitting in an old gymnasium in the Carolinas and talking to another performer in the place, Johnny Cash. The man in black told young Jim he would need to commit to being on the road 200 nights a year, or he should consider another line of work.

I knew right then, Jim recalls, *that I wanted to go home.*

Jim found a home at Heartland. He still plays a mean bass. At many of our company summits, Jim brings together Heartlanders from all around the United States to play music. At our company gatherings, they raise the roof.

We've learned at Heartland to give people wide roads, but high curbs. In other words, we provide plenty of independence, but we expect people to meet high standards of ethical behavior and professional accomplishment.

Not everyone is cut out to work in sales. We try to give our starting sales professionals plenty of coaching and guidance. We work to build confidence and we look for low-hanging fruit that can help beginners achieve some early success.

We offer signing bonuses to help people manage cash flow in the beginning. We also have a bridge compensation plan, which gives a salesperson a guaranteed salary for a fixed period of time as long as they work hard every day.

But sometimes it just doesn't work out. It means parting ways. We're not doing anyone a favor by keeping them in a job they hate and that makes them feel like a loser. In these cases, it's better to let them find another path. They're not a bad person. They're simply in the wrong line of work. Hopefully, they'll go find some other kind of pursuit and really find what makes them happy and successful.

We believe in people who have their priorities straight. I tell my employees: If you think it's important to be at home having dinner with your family, then you shouldn't be working late every night.

That credo helped us land a sales pro named Justin Volrath. He was living in Iowa, where his family had shut down a plumbing business, and he had gone into a job selling real estate.

When his dad would call on a Saturday to invite him to watch the Iowa Hawkeyes (Justin's favorite) or the Iowa State Cyclones (his dad's team), Justin usually had to decline because he was working an open house.

His wife, Nini, his high school sweetheart, would spend weekends with relatives, a close-knit family of Laotian immigrants, and Justin had to miss out.

His daughter, Belle, would sing in concerts at her elementary school, and the dad would miss her performances. He also missed the baseball games of his son, Justin Jr., who was then a nine-year-old playing for a team called the Four Mile Storm.

Justin's son had dreamed of being a catcher, but the coaches played him in the outfield instead. One lucky day, the little boy got his big chance: He was assigned to play behind home plate.

That night, when Justin came home from his real estate work, his son shared the big news.

Aw, Dad, he told him, *I wish you could have been there to see it.*

The boy explained that other dads at the game had helped him get his catcher's gear on and off.

It nearly broke the dad's heart.

Now a sales manager at Heartland, Justin sees his daughter's concerts and watches his son on the field. His boy is now playing football. The dad not only sees his games, he even attends the afternoon practices.

• • •

A lot of people find their soul mates at Heartland. Even in the card transaction processing business, there's no stopping romance. One of our top executives, Anne Mellin, a division manager, is married to another division manager, Sue Schoenfeld. They were wed on Cannon Mountain in New Hampshire.

Anne has said she has always felt *completely accepted* at Heartland. I should hope so. Any company who wouldn't welcome her talents, or Sue's, isn't a very intelligent enterprise.

It is a lucky CEO who has people like them as employees—and friends. On one difficult day in July of 2014, I would walk with Jill, who was in tears, toward a scene of destruction. Anne and Sue were there to comfort us, with their arms outstretched.

. . .

For a long time, I had wanted to find something that would symbolize the important roles played by the most valuable team members at Heartland. I looked around for something special, but just couldn't find anything that was special enough. I looked at all the traditional gifts and mementos—crystal trophies, plaques, luggage, watches, trips. I scoured catalogue after catalogue but couldn't find what I was looking for.

Then one day, while I was reading a copy of *USA Today*, I saw a picture of a hiker who was leaning back, sitting on the top of a mountain. You could tell that he was tired, but deeply satisfied that he had *made it*.

With the help of our chief marketing officer, Mike Hammer, we commissioned a painter, Charles H. Pabst, to paint on canvas what I wanted to symbolize.

We now award a painting by Pabst to employees at each of three important milestones of service at Heartland.

The first is called *Out of the Woods*, and it depicts a hiker who has found a clearing in the wilderness above the trees, looking down at the confusion from the recent past.

The second is called *Inspiration Point*, and illustrates a person who has reached a very high peak with the highest peak still far above.

The third painting is called *Journey's Reflection*, and shows a person sitting atop a mountain, looking out on a glorious view of the woods and the peaks and valleys below.

We have given out thousands of these paintings. It is a testament to having so many employees who have climbed such great heights. The winners of those paintings built Heartland. These employees came from all kinds of backgrounds, some quite modest, and now more than 150 of them have earned more than a million dollars working in a job they love.

8

LEADERSHIP FROM THE RANKS

We live in an age of the cult of personality. It's true in Hollywood, sports and the world of business, too.

In some cases, CEOs of some of America's biggest companies have become celebrities akin to rock stars. The success of companies is often seen as the result of a single genius at the helm.

It's not so simple.

Nancy Kane, of the Harvard School of Business, is among those who caution against this type of thinking: *Only so much of a company's success can be credited to one person.*

Investing too much importance in a leader is, quite literally, risky business. By definition, the CEO is temporary. Everyone is going to die.

What ultimately defines a company is its culture. Mary Frances Carr taught me that nobody is too important to learn from someone else, no matter the job rank. When we ignore the enormous reservoir of talent and potential among any employees, we are missing great opportunities for leadership.

People at every level of an organization have important insights. If they are given a voice, they will help find solutions and generate new opportunities. In doing so, they play an important role in leading the company. It doesn't matter if they have a corner office or if they are sweeping a floor.

Our company's debacle with the service center—when people were working in cage-like cubicles—illustrated the perils of management that was overly top-down. Listening to our service center employees, who had some great ideas about ways we could improve the operation, demonstrated the power of collegiality.

Gordon Bethune, who led a turnaround at Continental Airlines, talked often about the importance of treating workers as colleagues.

You can't treat your employees like serfs, he told an interviewer. *You have to value them. I know if I piss off a mechanic, he's going to take twice as long to fix something. That's Human Nature 101. If employees are hostile, they'll go out of their way to screw you.*

The *New York Times* has long been regarded as an authority when it comes to explaining the world's vexing issues. But in the early 2000s, the *paper of record* was experiencing some big problems under its own roof.

A new executive editor, Howell Raines, was the new sheriff in town, and he made it clear that he was going to be laying down the law. He made sweeping personnel changes. It was his intent, he told the staff, to *raise the competitive metabolism* of the organization.

To many of the staffers at the *Times*, a newspaper that has won far more Pulitzers than any other, it sounded like Raines didn't think they were working hard enough.

Raines cast aside some highly respected editors and reporters, and promoted a circle of his favorites. One of them was a protégé named Jayson Blair, a reporter then still in his 20s.

Before long, editors at the paper were discovering a series of fabrications and plagiarisms in Blair's work. One of the editors, Jonathan Landman, fired off an email to higher-ups:

We have to stop Jayson from writing for the Times. Right now!

When revelation of the misdeeds became public, the integrity of the newspaper came under attack. Blair resigned, and the staff rose up against Raines, who was seen as an autocrat bent on changing the long-established customs of a proud institution, what one staffer described to the *New Yorker* as *this precious thing we hold in common.*

In a meeting with some 600 *Times* staffers, employees seethed about the damage to the paper. Raines was soon forced to resign.

The episode at the *Times* showed the importance of a company's culture and ethos. This was a revolt from within, driven by employees who felt a sense of ownership in the institution, and an obligation to speak up when a leader is seen as violating its fundamental tenets.

. . .

In today's age of virtual reality, authenticity is worth more than ever.

That's why a certain memo at Heartland gave me concern.

One of our brightest young stars had issued a memo sprinkled with so much sugar that it came off as saccharine.

I zipped him an email.

This is a coaching moment, I explained, so that he understood this was serious. *I am recommending you reconsider using words that are overblown and obvious exaggerations...it hurts your credibility... call it like you see it...it will make you authentic in the eyes of your peeps, something that is gold when you need it.*

The progress of this leader matters deeply to me. Among other talented leaders at Heartland, he might be a candidate to take my place one day. Grooming leadership is one of the key responsibilities of a leader—and one of the most neglected.

If I cannot see Heartland without Robert Carr, I'm being worse than selfish. I'm damaging the sustainability of the company I love.

9

A DAMN GOOD PLACE TO WORK

If you're in charge, you can get away with spouting all sorts of absolute nonsense, and you're apt to be told:

What a great idea!

That's the ticket!

You're absolutely right!

So when people at Heartland would tell me that our company was a wonderful place to work, I appreciated the kind words. Because of my background, many Heartland employees know that building great jobs is one of my most important missions. So when someone tells me *I love my job*, I can never be 100 percent sure if they really mean it, or if they are just sucking up to the boss.

I also knew that most were unlikely to tell me anything else. What they might be thinking to themselves, or saying at home at the kitchen table, that could be a whole other kettle of fish.

I wanted to get an unvarnished look at how our people really see the company and their job.

A San Francisco company, called the Great Place to Work Institute, conducts confidential surveys of employees at businesses around the world. These questionnaires are designed to measure the levels of trust and satisfaction among employees. Their best-known ranking is published by *Fortune* magazine, the *100 Best Companies to Work For.*

If we were going to participate in the survey, we would be required to allow our employees to share whatever they thought about Heartland—good or bad—without being identified.

Would we be willing to do that?

I jumped at the chance.

As I told some colleagues: *Let's see how we really stack up.*

The survey worked this way:

We were to submit to the research institute the contact information for all of our employees: top executives, clerical staff, technicians, sales professionals—everyone who drew a paycheck from Heartland. The analysts would choose one-third of those workers, entirely at random, and reach out to them.

Heartland employees who were contacted could say as much or as little as they wished about anything at all. Or they could take a pass on the whole thing.

In a company-wide email, I announced that we were taking part in the survey. I stressed that the process was optional and confidential, and that people should answer the questions honestly.

When the results arrived a few months later, I opened the email and stared at the screen.

I was stunned.

The results showed that a whopping 87 percent of our employees in the survey rated Heartland as *a great place to work*.

I wasn't sure I could believe it. Could this really be accurate? Every organization has people who are unhappy and frustrated. Some are even hostile. It's human nature.

For virtually nine of every ten people to describe Heartland as a great company...Wow!!!

I called the PR department.

What does this mean? How do we compare?

I wanted them to do some exploring and put these numbers into some kind of context.

We quickly got feedback: It was a terrific score. Our employees had given Heartland rave reviews!

I was so proud I told anyone within earshot.

People generally assume that the day Heartland went public on the New York Stock Exchange was the most fulfilling experience of my career.

It wasn't.

Seeing the score on this survey was, in some ways, even more satisfying.

I arranged to purchase an analysis of the survey, as well as the employee comments collected by the Great Place to Work Institute.

The survey was known as the *Trust Index*. It was designed to measure how people feel about a company, and how they feel about their various relationships within the workplace culture.

When the package of comments finally arrived, I settled into a chair in the library at my home, near the fireplace. I felt as if I were a child opening Christmas presents.

As an entrepreneur, I had been through so many missteps, bad judgments and outright failures. I had lost a lot of good years trying to recover from the mistakes I made in the '70s and '80s just to get back to square one.

As I sat and read the comments, I thought about how they counted for so much. This was about the stuff that really mattered.

I had always wanted to build a successful company where employees could prosper financially, intellectually *and* emotionally. In the employee comments, I saw a validation of many things I had struggled to achieve in my career.

As I read some of the comments, I grew emotional. I wished my mother had been around to read them with me.

People in this company truly care about each other.

Working for Heartland is like working with a family.

This is the only place I have worked where I can express my personal beliefs.

No one judges you, even when you have personal issues.

The survey found that 87 percent of employees thought it was a great place to work—not 100 percent. A few stressed that they were not drinking our company Kool-Aid.

Going to a training session at Heartland feels like a bad cult meeting.

I got a kick out of that one.

For the most part, the complaints focused on the cost of health insurance—I can't disagree with that—and nepotism. It's true that we have more than a few people working at Heartland who are related to other employees. Some of that came about through our colleagues getting married to one another.

A few people complained that our printers needed to be upgraded. Someone wrote that the parking lot was too far from the entrance.

The general tenor of the comments, however, left little doubt that most people felt pretty darned good about working for the company.

We sometimes fall short. Not everyone at Heartland is enamored with everyone else. There are disputes and personality differences that can be harmful if they are left to fester.

In the case of one work relationship, the level of animosity grew to a dangerous level. They were really butting heads. It was potentially harmful to the company. Something had to be done about these two characters.

One of them was a Heartland leader. The other was me.

We had disagreed about plenty of moves within the company. He had severely criticized some of my decisions, and had even taken swipes that I regarded as severe, even belittling. I am certain that he felt the same way about some of my comments.

So, as CEO, why didn't I just fire the guy?

Here's why. He's good at his job. He's trustworthy. He tells me what he really thinks.

What matters most is that people are an important asset for Heartland. If it happens sometimes to be a pain in the neck to Bob Carr, well, it could be worse.

Throughout history, the best of leadership has drawn on the understanding that there is value in learning from those holding strong views with which we disagree. As long as you don't kill each other and, most importantly, as long as you trust one another's motivations and intentions, it can be very productive to work with adversaries.

And it's crucial not to think that all good or important ideas are passed down from on high—from the CEO, the board of directors, the top managers. Effective entrepreneurs look everywhere for good ideas. It might be a peer. It might be an assistant. Maybe it's an intern. It could even be a family member. It's important to have our assumptions and conventions challenged.

Being listed on the pages of *Fortune* as one of the nation's *100 Best Companies to Work For* would have been a great honor. It was not to be. We narrowly missed being chosen.

One of the factors that hurt us was our participation rate. While more than half of our employees took part in the survey, the percentage wasn't as high as it was at some other companies. We hadn't done very much to promote the survey, and it showed.

Missing out on the *Best Companies* list was a disappointment. But it wasn't demoralizing. Falling short simply meant we had more work to do. We needed to focus on more ways to make Heartland an even better place to work.

At a gathering of business leaders, I listened as a fellow started talking about the importance of employee engagement. The man was singing my song.

We talked. He has a company called The Energy Project. The upshot was that I hired him to help our employees become healthier, happier and maybe even more prosperous.

We identified thirty employees in the company, and brought them together to learn more about the importance of energy, health and life balance.

Early research by the Energy Project analysts revealed a couple of major themes in our company. The good news was that our people held a high degree of respect for the organization. The bad news was that a lot of our people felt overwhelmed and stressed.

Some of that is perception. My work load is too high. I'll bet your work load is too high. That's life. You get as much done as you can, and you try not to lose sight of what's really important, both at work and at home.

Some of it is simple. It's important to exercise, get enough sleep and eat well. Being simple, however, doesn't make it easy.

My own physical habits, according to the experts, left much to be desired. If it's got sugar in it, I probably like it.

As I listened to our energy experts at the session, one message seemed especially resonant: *Clarify your values.* If we don't know what we believe is right, we are lost. The truth is, we almost always do know in our hearts what is right.

Ed Cohee, one of our sales leaders from Kansas, said it best:

What's right is right, even when no one else is doing it; and what's wrong is wrong, even when everyone else is doing it.

I don't believe in stress, at least not in the way that stress is usually described. To put it another way, I think stress is optional.

As I see it, stress is the result of doing things you know that you shouldn't be doing. I don't mean just the obviously bad things, like lying or stealing. I'm talking about behavior that doesn't align with our values and aspirations.

If you don't believe in what you do, the way you're living your life, your performance will almost certainly suffer. And it's not a very pleasant way to live.

It was while battling cancer that the writer Winifred Gallagher came to a profound insight: *The skillful management of attention is the sine qua non of the good life and the key to improving virtually every aspect of your experience, from mood to productivity to relationships.*

She boiled it down to this: Our world amounts to the elements we choose to focus on.

Long before he became president, Bill Clinton said he made use of his ability to compartmentalize his world. By dividing the parts of his life into distinct psychological containers, he was able to focus on the task at hand, aware that he would otherwise be overwhelmed with all the disparate voices tugging for his attention.

As a child growing up in a chaotic household, I learned this method of coping at a very early age. If I had spent too much of my time dwelling on my father's sullen moods and his hurtful words, it would surely have detracted from activities that I *could* control.

I decided as a boy that while I had to *hear* a lot of his nonsense, I didn't have to act on it, and I surely didn't have to *believe* it.

10

WHEN CONFIDENCE TAKES A HIT

I've always been a little cocky. Even in the worst of times. I believed I was smart enough and would work hard enough to make things work eventually. When the picture looked grim for my career or my business, as it did many times, I still felt certain I could think and work hard enough to find my way. I thought I was pretty good at making lemonade out of lemons.

It helps enormously to have people in your life who believe in you, and I have had that good fortune, first with my mother, and later with my wife, Jill, who stood with me for so long. Jill considered herself as my partner, as well she should.

When our financial circumstances were tight, if she ever doubted me, she did not tell me. There were times, naturally, that she wondered if my dream of making a success in business was worth all of the trouble, or whether I should simply settle for a good, secure job working for someone else.

Growing up, I did pretty well in school. But I wasn't one of the best. I was an A minus, B plus kind of student. There were some students who were truly brilliant, or so it seemed to me. They tended to come from 'good families,' homes that were relatively tranquil, or at least had a quiet place to study.

After graduating from the University of Illinois with two degrees, landing a job at Parkland College and finding some success in the local business community, it began to dawn on me that maybe I was smarter than I thought.

And maybe I wasn't.

In fundamental ways, my early success was too much, too soon—especially for a working-class kid with a chip on his shoulder. I still had a lot to learn. I didn't yet know what I didn't know. And I surely thought I knew some things that I didn't.

As Mark Twain warned, *It ain't what you don't know that gets you in trouble, it's what you know that just ain't so.*

In the business world, a well-founded and *authentic* sense of confidence, based on reality and grounded in a value system, is one of the most important attributes you can have. In fact, it might be the single most valuable asset in life. At one conference I was introduced as the *most authentic CEO in America.* I consider that to be some of the highest praise I have ever received.

Without confidence, it's easy to lose your way, even if you have an abundance of talent. One of the most public and remarkable displays of debilitating self-doubt involved a baseball player for the New York Yankees named Chuck Knoblauch.

An All-American for Texas A&M, he won honors as the American League Rookie of the Year in 1991 and later garnered enough votes to be inducted into Cooperstown. For many years, he racked up lofty batting averages and earned a reputation as a great fielder. For his defensive prowess, he won the coveted Gold Glove award in 1997.

But by 1999, he was succumbing to doubts about his ability to make even the simplest of plays. My son Ryan and I sat in the grandstands of Yankee Stadium during one game and watched one of his worst meltdowns. He fielded a routine ground ball, and threw it so far over the first baseman it hit the head of the mother of a sportscaster, Keith Olbermann, who was sitting behind the dugout.

The player's doubt became almost crippling. In this game against the Chicago White Sox, he committed three errors in six innings, and then took himself off the field. With the game still in progress, he fled the dugout and left Yankee stadium in his street clothes.

Confidence isn't the same as bluster. It isn't conceit. It isn't a matter of thinking we're always right, or that somehow we're better than others. That kind of thinking can be delusional. And it can easily translate to some pretty obnoxious behavior.

Confidence doesn't mean being foolhardy. If anything, it means you have assessed the risks and made plans for whatever might happen. *What is the worst that can happen?* you ask yourself. *If I'm wrong, can we survive?*

At almost every turn, a sense of confidence has sustained me. When the security data breach threatened to ruin Heartland, I agonized through a long and sleepless night of worry and doubt, but I was steady by the next day. I believed I knew the way to wage a campaign that would save the company.

No matter the circumstances, I have never looked in the mirror and seen a man with a broken sense of confidence.

Until the day Jill told me she no longer wanted to be married to me.

. . .

When it comes to marriage, I am a failure. That's not my opinion. It's a matter of record. I have been married to two smart women, and both ultimately found me lacking.

Jill and I met just before Christmas of 1977. I was thirty-two and she was nineteen.

She had just been kicked out of Illinois College, in the middle of her sophomore year, because her parents had neglected to pay her tuition. She and her parents were moving into an apartment a floor above mine in the apartment building on East Street.

I was scraping along, getting over the divorce from my first wife, Susan, and trying to find some success in business. I was also contemplating a position on the City Council.

I was immediately taken with Jill. She was very smart and had an easy laugh. She was beautiful and trim and if you looked at a picture of her, you'd swear it was Mia Farrow.

Jill's dad, Bill Jackson, had been a coach of mine in high school. I wasn't yet very tall or strong in my sophomore year, and Coach Jackson cut me from the basketball team. I would later joke that I got even with him by marrying his daughter.

We married in 1980 at the First Congregational Church in Lockport, where each of us had been baptized and confirmed. We couldn't afford a real wedding reception, so we gathered in the church basement for cake and coffee.

We lived in Lockport for several months, but the clients in my fledgling computer software business were mostly in Kansas and Oklahoma, and that's where I was spending most of my time. So we moved to Oklahoma.

Jill helped in the business by teaching clients about my software and how to use computers, since PCs were virtually brand new in those days.

Our son, Ryan, was born in 1982. Kelly came along in 1984. Emmalee was born in 1990.

In 1983 we moved back to the Lockport area because Mildred, Jill's mother, learned that she had cancer. We got into financial straits by living in a house that was too big and expensive. It was my fault, but she never blamed me.

Jill understood the business challenges I faced. She was on my side. She lived frugally. She told me she believed in me and that she knew everything was going to be all right eventually. And I was certain that we'd find success, too.

After we moved to Florida in 1986, she went back to college and finished her degree in counseling at the University of South Florida. She graduated Phi Beta Kappa. In her entire academic career, from grammar school through college, Jill only once earned a grade below an A—and that was before junior high.

With the kids, Jill was present and in-the-moment—available to them intellectually and emotionally. While she offered strong support to me and our children, she had no appetite for being a disciplinarian. Jill was no shouter or spanker, not even close.

She was easygoing 100 percent of the time. I consider myself to be easygoing most of the time—but not always. I will fight for my principles. Jill does not fight.

When success did come, money did not change Jill. We were able to travel to interesting places around the world. We bought and refurbished the Wilson home in Princeton. And we started the *Give Something Back Foundation*, which primarily sends poor and working-class kids to college. We also established a teacher recognition program in Lockport in the name of her dad, William, and her mother, Mildred.

One day Jill told me that she was changing her religion and had joined the Catholic church. Our kids were all grown and away from the house. She was no longer interested in the business. We had grown apart. We had been partners for more than thirty years. I felt that I had been a good partner. I guess I was wrong.

· · ·

I believe that most busy people face an occupational hazard when it comes to personal lives. We become so engaged in work, travel, trying to achieve success. We feel responsible for all of the people in our lives who depend on us.

When you achieve successes, you try to share the limelight. But a smart partner can tell when it is forced or shallow. Jill would later explain that company business and social demands came to dominate our life in ways that she found overwhelming. Like a lot of business leaders, I rise early and work long hours before dinner. Anyone who knows me is familiar with my emails that sometimes ping long before the sun rises.

I do know this much: When you lose your life partner, it can take a hell of a toll on your self-image. Over the next few months, I lost about forty pounds, and I certainly wasn't on any diet. I was just shrinking.

Neither of us succumbed to the cliché of the spiteful, bitter ex-spouse. We are still friendly to one another and nothing—nothing—could ever shake our shared passion for our children.

Through all of it, Heartland has continued to succeed and prosper. In the toughest of personal times, I still worked with every fiber to do the very best that I could.

Many of my colleagues had little idea about the dissolution of my marriage. One of them who did know described me at a gathering as *the most resilient CEO on the planet*, given the breach, the loss of a fortune in stock and the breakup of my marriage, all within two years.

I couldn't help but be a bit amused by the description. At times, I didn't feel so resilient. But I guess none of us can see what's going on inside someone else's heart and mind.

In staying committed to my work, despite the hard times at home, I am certainly not special. Anguish is part of the bargain of life. I know that plenty of people at every level know what it's like to get up and go to work, even when it hurts, even when it feels as though your personal life has been rocked by an earthquake. The same is true of our customers, of course, and it's true for the people in your world, as well.

It's worth remembering the old saying: *Be kind, for everyone you meet is fighting a hard battle.*

11

THE COLOR OF MONEY

In the 1960s, my father often vowed he would never sell our house to a black family.

He didn't use the word *black*, of course, or *colored*, or the conventional term of the day, *Negro*.

He used the far more sinister word.

The presence of black people, he explained, would hurt property values.

Our neighborhood of Homer consisted of about a dozen small homes on two streets in the countryside. Our house was overcrowded and out of date. We still relied on coal for heat.

The place down the street was a wreck. It had an outdoor toilet and looked like it would fall down in a strong wind. The house across from that belonged to a family that was desperately poor and troubled with drug problems. The father had died of an overdose—something that was rare in those days.

This was the paradise that my father vowed to protect from any possible invasion of African Americans.

As a boy of fifteen or sixteen, I had the temerity to challenge him to defend his bigotry.

My father had a job at Argonne National Laboratory, working among people of all races, including black employees who certainly had more income and education than anyone in our neighborhood.

So I asked him a simple question:

You wouldn't sell the house to a black nuclear engineer from Argonne with a Ph.D.?

He replied firmly:

No.

I came at him again: *You'd rather have a white neighbor with an eyesore of a house than a black family who would build the best house in the area?*

That's right.

This was hardly the first time I had observed prejudice under my roof. But it was possibly the most vivid example I had yet experienced of the utter illogic—the nonsense—of racism.

Blinded by skin color, people like my father were willing to do things that ran absolutely against their own interests.

These were the years before the civil rights movement. As a white adult who used racial epithets, my father was not a rarity. For that matter, plenty of kids my own age talked that way.

I had never known a black person while in elementary school. In high school, however, I struck friendships with African American kids through sports. I remember Early DeLoach, a halfback on the football squad. Eddie Duncan could catch passes that most of us could never get near. I especially admired our basketball team's star center, Bobby Gadsen. On and off the court, Bobby had a terrific personality. No matter the situation, he was calm and collected.

In school, I became the number one singles player on the tennis team and I had been the fastest backstroker on the swimming team. But I also had a part-time job reporting on high school sports for the *Joliet Herald News*. It was a pretty cool gig for a teenage boy.

As a stringer, I took notes as I covered the basketball and football teams and track meets. After the games, I would call in to the tough-talking, smoke-filled newsroom on Oneida Street in Joliet to deliver my account of the action to an editor. I would drive to Joliet every week to write the pre-game and post-game articles.

A couple of years earlier, before I grew, I had been cut from the basketball team. As a reporter, however, I had become something of a member of the team. Many of the players on the sports teams were African American. When it came to people who were involved in sports, I learned, race was not such a big deal. When you're running down a football field, I guess, the color of the guy blocking for you doesn't seem all that important.

The same was true of the reporter covering the game. You share a lot of experiences, tense moments and joking around. The football coach took a liking to me and let me stand on the sidelines with him during the games. Occasionally he asked me what play to call. That was cool. It also didn't hurt to be the fellow who could put a player's name and heroics into print.

Almost all of the blacks at school lived in a section called Fairmont. For all practical purposes, the neighborhood should have been part of Lockport. But the town leaders never deemed it necessary to include Fairmont as an official part of our municipality.

A generation later, in 1978, Lockport Township High School had a sensational basketball team. The Lockport boys' team won every single game. In one of the most remarkable runs in Illinois basketball history, the Lockport varsity squad went 33–0 and won the state championship. Most of the best basketball players were African Americans and they all lived in the Fairmont section.

By then, I had moved back to Lockport. I was still trying to make it in a career as a software developer. It's fair to say that I was not achieving quite the success of the Lockport basketball team.

The feats of the basketball squad inspired some proud days in Lockport. Jill and I were caught up in the excitement. We drove down to Champaign, my old stomping ground at the University of Illinois. We gleefully watched our local boys win the state title before cheering throngs at the cavernous Assembly Hall, in games so high-profile they were broadcast live by the Chicago-based superstation WGN.

I was still interested in politics in those days. Not quite thirty-three, I was serving on the City Council in Lockport. As the chair of the finance committee and mayor pro tem, I had some measure of political power, or so I thought. I was determined to right what I considered to be an historic wrong. I wanted to annex the Fairmont neighborhood into the city of Lockport.

I viewed it was the fair and right thing to do. By this time, people of goodwill shared a belief in racial equality, or at least talked as if they did. And now the basketball team had brought us all together.

Everyone was beaming about the remarkable feat of the team. It was time to bring the neighborhood into the family, so to speak, to make it a full-fledged part of the city. If ever there was a time to do it, it seemed to me, this was it.

As I would learn, however, we hadn't made the kind of progress I had thought. I approached one alderman after the next, all of them white, and the responses I received were the same. Each assured me that, while they personally favored the incorporation of Fairmont into Lockport, their constituents were just not ready for it. They naturally couldn't publicly support any such measure.

In other words, Fairmont was good enough to supply sports stars that allowed Lockport to bask in the refracted glory of a state championship. But the neighborhood still wasn't good enough to be part of *us*.

It was racism, pure and simple.

Annexing Fairmont would actually have brought us money from an initiative created and backed by President Richard Nixon, known as *Special Revenue Sharing for Urban Community Development*. We would have been eligible for grants to upgrade the water and sewer department. The city coffers would have been enriched.

But racism was more powerful than self-interest, just as it had been in the case of my father.

Exasperated and frustrated by the episode, I soon decided not to run for re-election. I ended my short-lived career as a politician.

. . .

Watching my own children, meanwhile, fills me with hope about relations between people of different backgrounds.

When my son, Bob, was in college, he took some guff for considering joining a fraternity that was largely Jewish.

It didn't stop him. He joined the fraternity. And he loved it. More than twenty years later, his fraternity brothers are still among his closest friends.

He would later meet Melissa, a lovely young Hispanic woman. He didn't worry that they had come from different ethnic heritages. He was in love and she was too. And so they married. Melissa is the only person with a Ph.D. in the history of the Carr family.

Years later, I was filled with pride when I received an email of gratitude out of the blue from Bob. He thanked me for teaching him at an early age the importance of treating people equally, no matter their race, religion or the size of their bank account.

It was a long time ago, he wrote, *but I remember the message pretty clearly.*

. . .

At Heartland, we have employees of all backgrounds, among them African Americans, Latinos and Asians. Our chief financial officer is Jordanian.

We have a long way to go in achieving the level of diversity that I'd like to see. To put it plainly, Heartland, like a lot of other technology-based companies, skews too white and male.

Women today make up only 18 percent of computer science majors. We must find ways to propel that number. Hopefully, the *Give Something Back Foundation* can help a bit.

For a business, there are bottom-line advantages in becoming more culturally and racially polyglot. As the face of America changes, and markets become increasingly global, a diverse workforce can more adeptly reach customers of all kinds.

Louis Huang, a Heartlander, could speak barely a word of English when he arrived in California from his native China a decade ago. Even now, he works hard to master the language and the customs of his adopted country.

He watches television shows and movies as a way to acquaint himself with idioms and the way words are pronounced. At night, he attends a community college.

With his communications challenges, Louis might not be pegged as someone who would be a valuable asset for a business when it comes to working with the public.

That would be shortsighted. As a sales professional at Heartland, he is achieving success that grows by the day.

I'm living the American Dream, he said.

In Los Angeles, Louis has cultivated a client base of Chinese-speaking people who run stores and restaurants. He can earn their trust, in part, because he can speak their language.

To put it another way, a young Asian immigrant like Louis Huang brings a piece of business to Heartland that some white executive like Robert Carr could not.

12

THE KIDS ARE ALL RIGHT

Has any generation been more marginalized than the Millennials?

Born in the 1980s and 1990s, this is a group of people who have come in for a lot of bashing.

The litany is tired and familiar.

Young people feel entitled. They lack work ethic. They are self-absorbed. They are apathetic. They grew up in a trophy-for-all world and think they should be treated like champions!

In some quarters, young people have been portrayed as nothing less than a threat to civilization.

Consider the title of a widely discussed book about the Millennials by Mark Bauerlein: *The Dumbest Generation: How the Digital Age Stupefies Young Americans and Jeopardizes Our Future.*

And then there's the *Time* magazine cover story in 2013, *The Me Me Me Generation.*

The story contains the following quote: *Not only do Millennials lack the kind of empathy that allows them to feel concern for others, but they even have trouble intellectually understanding others' points of view.*

It's just so much bull.

The young people I see joining our company demonstrate a sense of purpose, a superior set of technological skills, and an eagerness to get along with other people.

An information technology trade group, CompTIA, conducted a study of workplaces and found that Millennials were *more* likely than other age groups to work collaboratively.

When it comes to credit card use, young people today don't handle financial debt quite like the mature folks of the generation before them.

The *kids*, it turns out, behave much more responsibly.

A Federal Reserve Bank report in 2014 found that people under twenty-one were significantly less likely to be delinquent in credit card payments than were those in middle age.

According to a study by Andra Ghent of Arizona State University, people in the age group between forty and forty-four were twelve percentage points more likely to be at least ninety days delinquent on credit card bills than were the nineteen-year-olds.

You read that right. Young people as a group have shown *greater fiscal discipline* than older people.

The Millennials have served valiantly, both in civilian causes and the military. I deeply respect the sacrifices made during World War II by the Greatest Generation, as Tom Brokaw has dubbed my parents' era. But it's important to recognize the many thousands of young people who have served the nation in war duty since 2001.

Many have served tour after tour after tour, even as much of the rest of America had little skin in the conflicts. The battle in Afghanistan became the *longest war in American history*, and our forces included troops who were kindergarteners when terrorists attacked the World Trade Center.

Compared to their parents' generation, young people today are less likely to smoke cigarettes, engage in risky sexual behavior or drive while drunk. It's my hunch that plenty of Millennials have watched some of the choices made by the parents—and decided to go another path.

This is a generation of people who think for themselves. A Pew Research Center survey in 2014 of people age eighteen to thirty-three found that 50 percent regard themselves as political independents. Three in ten do not consider themselves affiliated with any particular religious group.

It is also the most racially diverse generation in American history, with people of color numbering 43 percent. These are people who have grown up being more accepting of differences.

A lot of ink has been spilled about this generation's supposed preoccupation with materialism and comfort. It's an unfair charge. If people in the younger generation have anxiety about financial and career considerations, it is for good reason. They cannot afford to take anything for granted.

This is the first generation in the modern era to face higher levels of poverty and unemployment than the two previous generations, and lower levels of wealth and personal income.

Student debt today is crushing. Education loans now exceed $1 trillion, a sum that surpasses consumer debt. It is very difficult to buy a house with a monthly student loan payment of hundreds of dollars. Many college graduates today walk from commencement ceremonies to loan balances that exceed $100,000. And then there's the enormous federal debt that older Americans have long skirted, leaving the financial obligations on the shoulders of today's young people, or perhaps even their grandchildren.

It comes as no surprise, as studies have found, that more than half of all Millennials believe the Social Security system will run out of money by the time they retire.

Young people today understand that the competitive job market requires them to stand out from the crowd. They work furiously to groom resumes, take unpaid internships, volunteer for charitable causes.

The novelist Anna Quindlen, in a column titled, *An Apology to Graduates*, wrote of the pressure on young people to compete and succeed: *Your college applications look like resumes for middle-level executives*, she observed. *How exhausted you must be.*

Despite the burdens, young people are holding up well. In every sphere of life, including business, the energy of the Millennials is driving change for the better. Young people today bring a genuine commitment to a shared well-being, whether it is promoting a healthier planet or a thriving workplace.

The *reverse mentoring* trend is just one of the ways that organizations are drawing on the talents of Millennials to strengthen the workforce. Companies pair senior executives with tech-savvy young people, some of them just out of college. The goal is bringing the gray-heads up to speed with technology skills, including social media.

Millennials are going to lead the way, like it or not.

And I like it.

The values of the Millennials inspire confidence. Perhaps because they grew up in the shadow of the attacks of September 11, they see the world differently. They have a sense of what really matters, and what doesn't matter so much.

The Pew survey found the top three priorities of Millennials: Being a good parent, having a successful marriage and helping others in need.

At the bottom of the list, registering a scant 1 percent, was the desire to *become famous.*

The Stanford professor and philanthropy expert, Laura Arrillaga-Andreessen, has described Millennials as having *more social consciousness than any other generation.* She points to a study that shows 72 percent of college students in 2012 believe they can derive happiness by working for a firm that creates some sort of positive social impact. And she has noted that 65 percent of those young incoming workers would take a cut in pay to work for such a company.

Still other surveys show that more than 80 percent of Millennials say that making a difference in the world is more important than professional recognition. And 92 percent believe that businesses should be measured by more than profits.

Sign me up.

13

GIVING A KID A BREAK

In my senior year of high school, I read in the *Joliet Herald* that another student and I had been named $250 scholarship winners by the Lockport Woman's Club.

It came out of nowhere.

I hadn't applied for the award. I had never heard of the Lockport Woman's Club. And while I had done relatively well in school, squeezing into the top 10 percent of the class, there were plenty of kids in the class who were far better students. So the award was a big surprise.

It also seemed to me to be a pretty cool deal.

My picture was published in the newspaper. I received a plaque, engraved with my name, which would hang on my wall for many years. And I was given some needed money to put toward my schooling at the University of Illinois.

The most important part of the award, however, went far beyond the hardware and the cash. It was the lift it gave to my sense of self.

In a childhood where I had been taught that I was *just average*, as my mother reminded me, or a *sissy* and a *wise guy*, as my father had railed, the award made me think that someone thought I was special.

Looking back, I have a pretty good hunch that I was recommended for the award by a school counselor familiar with the circumstances in my home. I'll always be grateful.

The award showed the importance of a little recognition. Being celebrated for accomplishment, especially for young people who aren't always feeling good about themselves, can be a powerful motivator and a boon to self-confidence.

It's as if somebody has sized you up and declared, *Hey, you're really worth it!*

It struck me, even then, how much power another person or an organization has to make a kid smile—and dream. I remember thinking: *If I ever get rich, I'm going to do something like this for someone else who could use a boost.*

I'm going to give something back.

Nearly forty years later, I sent a letter to the Lockport Woman's Club and thanked them once again.

This time, I enclosed a donation to the club for $5,000.

It wasn't long before I received a reply.

You won't remember me, wrote a Mrs. LaTour, the president of the organization, *but you were a school safety guard when my girls were little.*

I remembered. Her daughters were among the cutest girls in school.

She said it was the first time in forty-eight years that any of the scholarship winners had given a donation back to the Woman's Club. She thanked me, and invited Jill and me to the club's annual banquet that summer in Lockport. As we would learn when we arrived, the event would mark the 100th anniversary of its founding.

During the dinner, I grew even more inspired by the club's mission to help students with small stipends for attending college.

I looked over at Jill, and whispered: *What do you say we give them $100,000?*

She smiled and nodded.

When it was my turn to address the crowd, I delivered my remarks and the surprise donation, a $100,000 check to the club to be used for five $20,000 scholarships for students in financial need at Lockport Township High School.

That was pretty much the beginning of the *Give Something Back Foundation*. We met the director of the school's foundation, a young man named Steve Cardamone. Steve and the Woman's Club would join us in selecting the recipients and would distribute the money.

Since 2003, our organization has been devoted to a mission of helping poor and working-class students pay for college. We are hoping the number of recipient scholars someday reaches 1,000 and more. And I am counting on some of the recipients to grow successful enough to give something back to the next generation.

◦ ◦ ◦

Many years had passed since I took out the wildly ambitious advertisement in the *New York Times* that announced my far-flung plan to run for president in 1996. Alas, it was a Clinton, and not a Carr, who won office that year. I long ago reconciled myself to the reality that I was not going to solve all of the world's ills.

But I knew that I could address *some* of the problems. The late writer and philosopher Carlos Castaneda summed it up this way: *If you only have enough extra money to help a couple of people, then go ahead and help those couple of people. If your means grow larger, you can expand your reach to others who could use a hand.*

The family is a good place to start. When I achieved some success, I opened a bank account in my mother's name and established a fund to pay out money to each of Mary Frances Carr's descendants and their spouses. In all, Jill and I distributed more than $6 million to my family and her friends and family members.

Great wealth had come upon us almost overnight. I established trusts for my children, with money to be dispensed to each of my daughters and sons in intervals at certain ages. The sums were substantial, but I put a cap on the amount.

As someone who has been rich and poor, I know it's better to be rich. But drowning in money at a young age can have drawbacks, too. It can thwart ambitions and desire and get in the way of a person from making a mark on the world in a positive way.

To decide what to do with the money, I attended some trust fund seminars. They talked a lot about planned estates and trust funds. There were plenty of heirs at these gatherings, mostly sons and daughters of dead rich guys, trying desperately to figure out what *Dear Old Dad* would want to be done with the loot.

I wasn't going to put my kids through that. And I didn't want to attach a bunch of strings to the trusts, either, as if trying to manage their lives from my grave.

I wanted the kids to make their own choices and find their own paths. They could use the money as they saw fit, and they would live with the consequences.

We called a family summit and talked about the privileges, as well as the perils, of being rich. Having money would make their lives easier in some ways, I told them, but it would make it more challenging in others.

Being wealthy would require them to make decisions that I never had to make. Like whether or not to work. That was not something I ever had to ponder. As a young man, if I wanted to eat, I needed to get a job—just like everybody else.

Not having to work seems like an extravagant option, and it is, but it can also lead to questioning one's purpose and value in life.

Having money would also mean that they would have no excuses. You often hear people complain that they stayed in a job they absolutely hated because they had no choice. They will tell you they might otherwise have been an accomplished painter or writer or teacher. But they were stuck. They can't be blamed for not pursuing their dream, they will tell you. They simply couldn't afford to take the chance.

My kids wouldn't have the luxury, if you can call it that, of explaining why they *just couldn't*.

With plenty of money, they *could* pursue dreams that didn't pay big financial dividends, but brought other rewards. And they have done so.

I am proud of the way my children have handled the money and the opportunities—along with the baggage—that comes with it.

I like to think of the foundation and our scholarship winners, who overcame hardship at home, as a family of sorts. You try to nurture the young in the nest, prepare them for the world, and then watch where they fly.

There are a lot of worthy causes I could have supported.

Why college scholarships?

In my own life, education made a difference of 1,000 percent. When I arrived at the University of Illinois, the world seemed to expand exponentially beyond the old limits, and so did my view of the horizons.

I arrived at college intending to become a high school math teacher, a respectable calling, but eventually found myself inspired to reach for goals far beyond my grasp.

Educational attainment is something that can be measured. For $20,000, we can put a student through college and likely change the course of a life. To me, that seems like a bargain.

There's also the multiplier effect of the investment, starting with the way it affects the families of the students.

Most of us who have experienced any sort of personal drama can understand that the family is a circle. All of us are connected. The joy and despair of any family member tends to affect the others.

So when a struggling family succeeds in sending a child to college, and later sits beaming from the bleachers on that glorious graduation day, it brings a sense of pride to mothers and fathers, and to grandparents, sometimes most of all, that they, too, have succeeded in life. And they are justified in sharing in that triumph, especially those who have navigated a life strewn with hurdles.

The graduation of a loved one also sends a message of possibility to siblings, cousins and friends. Look at my big sister, my little brother, my pal from the neighborhood—look what they have done! Maybe I can do that, too!

It is all a circle.

The foundation has been much of the most rewarding work of my life. I can relate to these kids. In our society, we frequently underestimate young people from modest and struggling backgrounds. We don't always appreciate the strength of character of these kids, not to mention their brainpower. There are a few bad apples, for sure, but most are good kids. They simply face daunting obstacles.

Back in the day, tuition was a few hundred bucks a year. I was able to put myself through school by working in the food service during my first few years. After that, I managed an Arby's restaurant for $2 an hour to pay the bills.

In today's world, you are not likely to be able to put yourself through school by flipping hamburgers. Unless you have a summer job robbing banks, you're probably going to need some help.

Our foundation focuses largely on kids who will be first-generation college students. A lot of them are also first-generation Americans. And many have never stepped foot on a college campus.

Most of these working-class kids have little in the way of social or business connections. Their families don't typically know people who can make a call and arrange an interview. I wanted these kids to build their own networks.

Through foundation events put together by Steve Cardamone and Bob Tucker, who comprise the foundation staff, and the *Give Something Back Foundation* Alumni group, I've watched these kids bond, commit to stick together, and realize they can draw support from one another when it counts.

Some of our scholarship winners are people who might have fallen through the cracks. Instead, they have worked and persevered and ultimately found a way to the commencement stage. And they have become members of society who are now in a position to help others at risk of slipping away.

It is all a circle.

14

DARING TO THINK DIFFERENTLY

———————————◆———————————

A picture of Ayn Rand hangs above my desk on the wall of my office.

I first read the libertarian philosopher while I was in graduate school. Rand upheld innovation and market capitalism and the capacity of human beings to achieve great things. She rejected both church and statism.

She stood for reason, individual rights and principled capitalism. Her philosophy championed the idea that you could do wonderful things and change the world for the better while also achieving great personal success.

Her view of the native intelligence and incredible capacity of human beings changed my life.

I had been brought up to believe that business people were inherently evil. I had been taught that the wealthy reached their goals by taking advantage of workers.

In Rand's blockbuster, *Atlas Shrugged*, I saw heroes who prospered through integrity, intellectual honesty and hard work.

And I saw villains, those who put a stranglehold on ambition and achievement, exerting control and repression. These teachings never really made sense to me, however.

I know that Ayn Rand is hugely out of fashion in many quarters. She is reviled by much of the academic elite. People who admire her philosophy are sometimes dismissed as sophomoric or scorned as heartless and self-centered. In politics, she is toxic.

In the 2012 campaign for the White House, Paul Ryan, the Republican nominee for vice president, was called out for his background as a Rand devotee. He had reportedly committed the sin of distributing her books as Christmas presents to friends. He even encouraged his staff to read her work. In the media, there was no shortage of snarky commentary about all of this.

Ryan promptly disavowed any connection to Ayn Rand. The clean-cut, Irish-Catholic politician declared that he soundly rejected her philosophy and—God knows—her outspoken atheism.

Dead for more than thirty years, Rand is still considered dangerous. In writing this book, some people cautioned me against even mentioning her name.

That might have been safest. But it would also be disingenuous. The truth is that Rand *was* a major influence in my life. So was Victor Hugo's *Les Miserables*, the multiple scientific and mathematical breakthroughs of John von Neumann and, of course, the incandescence of Albert Einstein.

Rand's philosophy of Objectivism and Ethical Egoism inspired me to leave safe jobs at Parkland College and the Bank of Illinois and try to change the world as an entrepreneur and then as a political leader. Her views helped me see that it was possible to craft a business that treated people with respect and offered people the opportunities to live up to their potential.

Unfortunately, her views these days have commonly been perverted by those who want to advance their own personal agendas in her name. Rand herself never intended for Objectivism to become an organized movement.

Some years ago, the executive director of the Ayn Rand Institute approached me and asked if I would be willing to help pay for the printing of Rand's slender paperback volume, *Anthem*, to be donated to high schools around the country.

I liked the idea of kids having the chance to read Rand, rather than simply hearing the usual clichés about her, so I agreed to pay for the printing of 100,000 copies. They cost a buck apiece.

For the books being shipped to schools, I wanted to write a foreword, in which I touched on Rand and Einstein as the leading meta-physicist and physicist, respectively, of the 20th century. Einstein's portrait long hung next to Rand's on my office wall.

But an influential member of the institute flatly rejected my foreword because I had *dared* to print the name of Albert Einstein in the same sentence as Ayn Rand. As I would learn, the world's greatest physicist was apparently persona non grata with the Ayn Rand Institute because he had espoused pacifist views.

The executive director of the Rand Institute came to my office to explain and rationalize the anti-Einstein stance.

I shook my head in astonishment, but paid for the books anyway.

As we talked, I mentioned that I had started an organization to help kids go to college, and I told him it was called the *Give Something Back Foundation*.

The Rand Institute leader said he found the name offensive. He was also suspicious of the mission itself.

He asked, *Do you feel guilty about something?*

I do not feel guilty. I get a lot for the money I give to the foundation. It is profoundly gratifying to help change the lives of so many young people. And it feels wonderful to be appreciated by the students and their families. Ayn Rand did not believe in altruism and neither do I. I don't give money to put kids through college out of altruism.

I do it because it is the best way to use my money and I get enormous enjoyment from it. If this makes me selfish, I plead guilty. I believe in John Stuart Mill's utilitarian principle— do what is best for the most people possible.

15

NOAH AND HIS DAD

As his father lay in the hospital bed, six-year-old Noah Birch, trying to comfort his dad, would reach up and tenderly swab the man's parched lips with moist sponges.

I remember the tall beds, said Noah, *and I remember the doctor explaining to me one day that my dad wasn't going to be with me for much longer.*

After his father died at age forty-five, little Noah decided he wanted to become a doctor himself someday.

His mom, Kathleen, was a social worker. A widow of modest means, she taught Noah and his older brother, Adam, that they simply couldn't afford some of the things that a lot of other kids took for granted.

From a young age, Noah knew the importance of doing whatever he could to pull his weight. In elementary school, he helped with his brother's paper route. In middle school, he worked at a flower shop. In high school, he bagged groceries after class and spent summers painting fire hydrants for the public works department in Lockport.

And he continued to dream about becoming a doctor.

Noah finished high school in 2002, a year before the foundation officially started. But when I heard about his circumstances, I called his mom, and then I called him.

Noah would become the first student to go to college with the help of a scholarship from the foundation.

As with a lot of the other young people in our program, I have stayed in touch with Noah. I remember the day he called to tell me he had been admitted to medical school at Loyola University in Chicago.

Now doing his residency at Northwestern Hospital, Noah has acted as a mentor for other working-class kids. He has spoken to groups of students and today serves on the board of directors of the foundation.

Noah earned his M.D., as well as a Ph.D. in molecular cellular biochemistry. He pursued the double-degree program because he wants to practice and do research. He wants to study malignancies.

I look back on my dad's death, he said, *and I realize there are still a lot of things in the medical field that we just don't understand.*

Noah is hoping to make discoveries that might someday spare another six-year-old kid from standing beside those tall hospital beds and watching a parent die.

College for Jodi Turnbough's children seemed like an impossible dream. The single mom worked days as a clerk in the records department at the Lockport Police Department. At night, she tended bar at a bowling alley called Strike 'N Spare.

When it came to her family's financial situation, she gave it to her children straight.

There is no money for college, she told them.

When her daughter, Alexandria, found out about our scholarship program, she decided to apply. She didn't bother her mother with the details. She knew she was busy working to pay the bills.

Without any help from home, Alexandria wrote an essay, contacted teachers for letters of recommendation, and sat through an interview in the scholarship competition.

Jodi will never forget the day the phone rang and she picked up and heard Alexandria shouting.

I could barely understand her, said the mom. *She kept screaming, 'I got it! I got it! I got it!'*

Alexandria had been selected as a winner. A top student, she is now finishing her studies at my alma mater in Champaign-Urbana.

She would never have been able to go to college otherwise— absolutely no way, her mom said. *I told her, 'For you, this is winning the lottery!'*

A few years later, Jodi's daughter, Abigail, now a junior at Lockport Township High School, also won a scholarship from the foundation.

To be eligible for the *Give Something Back Foundation* scholarships, students must come from households earning less than $50,000. They must qualify for a Federal Pell Grant, which offers a financial aid grant—usually $5,000 per year, a fraction of the total college cost—to kids from moderate and lower-income households.

Our scholarship program has been expanded from Lockport High School to twenty-one schools throughout Will County, south of Chicago, a polyglot of urban and suburban neighborhoods, gritty factories and rolling farm fields. The county's biggest city is Joliet, home of the state prison featured in the *Blues Brothers* movie with John Belushi and Dan Aykroyd.

To keep the scholarship, students must maintain a B average and stay out of trouble.

It is an expectation that you will remain a person of high character throughout your tenure with the Give Something Back Foundation, our handbook reminds students. *Specifically, that means make the right choices! What you do today, positively or negatively, affects the rest of your life. Violating the agreement that you signed or participating in activities (drinking, drugs, smoking or other poor behavior) that are counterproductive to you, your family or society can lead to dismissal from this program.*

We err on the side of forgiveness. If a student goofs up, but demonstrates sincere remorse, we have been known to give a second chance, and even a third one.

But accountability is part of our ethos. Choices come with consequences. Students have been dropped from the program for poor grades and rule-breaking. That means the loss of many thousands of dollars in scholarships, and perhaps an end of any chance to go to college.

It seldom comes to that, however, because we're on the lookout for early signs of trouble. Keeping kids in school is our central mission. It's all about the college graduation rate.

Steve Cardamone, the executive director of our foundation, has had some *come-to-Jesus* talks with students who seem to be flirting with self-destruction.

He doesn't mince words.

What the hell are you doing? he asked one bright young man who wasn't tending to his schoolwork. *Look at your poor mother!*

She's busting her rear end to give you a chance! You need to get it together!

The kid got it together.

As one student told Steve:

Sometimes I need a hug and sometimes I need a kick in the pants. This time I needed a kick in the pants. You need more from me, and I'm going to give it to you.

In many cases, a tender word of encouragement is the best medicine. When Steve picked up the phone one day, he could hear crying on the other end of the line. It was one of our past scholarship winners.

Steve wondered what terrible thing had happened.

It's a job interview, she explained, *and it could change my whole life.*

She was scared.

After rising above a tough family situation, making it into college and then succeeding in the classroom, this girl had arrived at Judgment Day.

At least that's how it seemed to her.

Steve calmed her down, gave her a little interview prep, reminded her of her considerable talents, and assured her that she was going to knock it out of the park.

And that's just what she did.

In addition to raising possibilities, we believe that the scholarship program has raised expectations in our schools in Will County. We noticed years ago that students from the elementary school in the Fairmont neighborhood, the neighborhood that brought Lockport its only state basketball title, were choosing vocational classes, or being steered to them.

Some of these bright kids were perfectly capable of attending a university. They might not have thought they could afford a four-year college. Maybe their advisers were thinking that way, too. Now they have their eyes on a prize.

We've heard similar reports throughout the county. Tim Ricketts, the principal at Reed-Custer High School in a fairly rural region, said he could point to kids who would not have considered college without the scholarship program.

You put a free ride to college on the table for a high school freshman, he said, *and that changes the way he or she looks at school, life, everything.*

Students are chosen for the scholarship in their freshman year of high school. They write 300-word essays about themselves, which gives us a snapshot of life at home. We interview each applicant and review grades.

We assign a mentor to each student—sometimes two or three mentors. We provide extra tutoring if needed. Grades are monitored each quarter. Students who fall below the required B average at mid-semester will receive a letter and meet with the foundation staff.

And we stay connected after the students leave high school. Our college students must write a short essay about their experiences after each academic year. Poor grades, including any mark lower than a C, means that a student will be disqualified from receiving any more scholarship money.

Patrick Ackerman was a very bright boy with severe Attention Deficit Hyperactivity Disorder. Even before kindergarten, his extreme impulsivity was causing worrisome behavior problems.

His mom, Kris, would take him to a program called Tuesday's Child, where the parents would gather in one room and the kids in another, both of them working on coping techniques.

With a lot of support and therapy, Patrick succeeded in the classroom and won a *Give Something Back Foundation* scholarship. As a student at Elmhurst College, he has achieved top grades, but he still sometimes struggled to fit socially with peers.

His worried mom called the foundation one day and asked for help. Patrick needed to talk to someone. So we arranged for a mentor to visit him promptly. Sometimes that's all any of us need—someone who will listen.

Patrick is going to make it. Now the head of a college group involved in public policy, he has emerged as a bona fide leader on campus.

He is already thinking about ways he can give something back.

He's building a fund from his textbook allowance from the foundation—money saved when he re-sells books at the end of semesters. He's donating it to the foundation, so even more kids can be helped.

It's nice to see the underdog come out on top, as his mom said, *and remember where he's been.*

. . .

Imagine being a kid who is promised a college scholarship— only to have it withdrawn.

It's outrageous. But it happens.

An organization will send a representative to Awards Day at a high school to stand behind a podium and wear a halo of generosity. But sometimes the money never reaches the student. If the organization's finances take a turn for the worse, the scholarship money vanishes.

It puts a family into a terrible dilemma, and dashes the hopes of a young student. It surely cannot do much to bolster a young person's trust in institutions and people.

It is a core principle of our foundation to guard against that kind of betrayal. When we make an award, the money is deposited in the bank for the student.

If I get run over by a truck tomorrow, all tuition promises will be kept.

That's partly how I got financially walloped during the breach and the ensuing stock price collapse. My money was in Heartland stock, and I didn't want to sell. I borrowed against the stock on margin, and put the money in a trust for the scholarships. My stock was sold to repay my loan.

I lost my shirt. But I wasn't about to jeopardize any of the money that had been promised for the college scholarships.

* * *

Over the years, we have adjusted course in the selection of our young scholars, to make as much impact as possible. When the foundation started, we followed the traditional scholarship model. We simply wrote checks to high-achieving students who demonstrated financial need—$20,000 awards to each student spread over four years of undergraduate study.

The students were selected during the senior year of high school, and were free to use the money to attend any college that would offer them admission. Some of our students went off to very prestigious colleges, including Harvard.

We achieved an astonishing graduation rate—more than 90 percent within four years. We questioned, however, whether we were making as much difference as possible. These were students with stellar grades, top scores and wonderful resumes. Some of our scholarship winners were kids who were going to find a way to college, whether we helped or not.

To make a bigger difference, we wanted to throw a lifeline to those students on the margins, the ones who were at real risk of giving up hope of going to college.

We also reconsidered the wisdom of waiting until a student's senior year to make our scholarship selections. By the last year of high school, students have already established academic habits, goals and expectations.

Studies show that most kids effectively decide whether to pursue the college path much earlier. The mindset they adopt as seventh and eighth-graders, and the choices they make, largely determine their academic destinations, even if they don't quite realize it at the time.

In changing course, we decided to select our scholarship winners closer to the beginning of high school. And we lay down conditions intended to motivate students to study hard and conduct themselves honorably through the high school years.

Our foundation created a businesslike approach to educational philanthropy. We negotiated with schools, offering a donation of $1 million. In exchange, we wanted deep discounts on tuition. We wanted to create as many scholarships as possible with the money.

We agreed to $1 million pacts with each of three schools: Lewis University in Romeoville, Illinois; the University of St. Francis in Joliet, Illinois; and Blackburn College in Carlinville, Illinois. Over time, the agreement will translate to full rides for 240 poor and working-class kids.

Students who choose Lewis or St. Francis, which are both located in Will County, where the kids live, will receive tuition waivers; students who choose Blackburn, a 'work' requirement school located in downstate Carlinville, about three hours from Will County, will also receive funding for room and board.

I personally discussed the $1 million check with each of the college presidents in our partnership. I wanted to look them in the eye and tell them how much these kids had overcome—and how much was at stake. It was important for me to know that these schools were truly committed to our program.

When I met these university leaders, I came away reassured. These were schools dedicated to reaching students who might not otherwise be sitting in a college classroom. I believe these kinds of partnerships can be replicated throughout the country.

At Lewis University, where I would later join the board, students learn to give something back as part of their education. They work with the homeless and the incarcerated. They help build houses in South America and they teach children in the poorest regions of America.

We try to incorporate that philosophy into every course, explained Brother James Gaffney, FSC, the president at Lewis. *If you're taking an accounting class, for example, you might earn service learning credit by volunteering to maintain the financial records for a nonprofit organization that cannot afford to hire a professional accountant.*

For students at Blackburn College, the connection between education and service is written into the contract. Blackburn is one of seven colleges in the nation that requires students to work as a way to keep costs down. Students staff the offices, tend the grounds and clean the buildings. Some of them even build the buildings.

This is not a school for affluent, privileged young people looking for a campus where they can just kick back and party. Each student is required to work a minimum of ten hours per week, with the wages going toward tuition costs. They are eligible to work up to twenty hours, if they choose, to earn some walking-around money.

Dr. John Comerford, the president at Blackburn, said his school isn't driven by a desire for greater prestige. At most institutions, where administrators can become obsessed with the *U.S. News* rankings, admissions officers are determined to court those student with top entrance exam scores. It helps boost the ratings.

Every other college in the country is going after the upper-middle-class kid with a score of 28 or higher on the ACT, he said. *I'm not going to win that race.*

As he sees it, those kids don't need Blackburn as much, anyway. They will find a place. It's the students on the margin, academically and economically, whose lives can be changed by attending his school.

That's a philosophy that fits my view. One of their proud alums, Bob Tucker, is now the associate director of the *Give Something Back Foundation.*

Getting to college is one thing. Staying is another.

Among students seeking a degree nationally, only 40 percent graduate within six years. Chuck Beutel, the vice president for admissions at the University of St. Francis, stressed his school's success in pushing students to the finish line, no small feat for so many of the students juggling a job and the demands at home.

He said that's why employers look so fondly on those who earn a degree. It's not just what students have learned about subjects. It's what they have demonstrated about themselves. Businesses themselves can teach the details about their companies and the duties they need to learn. They cannot teach character.

When it comes to cocktail chatter in certain social circles, schools like Lewis and St. Francis and Blackburn might not tend to win bragging rights. But their hard-working students know some things you don't learn in the Ivy League.

16

FINDING THE WAY HOME

———— ⦿ ————

When my son, Ryan, was a little boy, he struggled to find his way.

He was too heavy. At eight years old, he weighed eighty-eight pounds. He struggled with athletics. He wasn't interested in the same things as the other boys in his circle, many of whom came from military families at MacDill Air Force Base in Tampa.

What interested Ryan was reading. He would read any book you put in front of him.

I was the leader of his Cub Scout den. When it came time for the Pinewood Derby, I encouraged all of the kids to make their own race car. Many of the dads, regardless, went ahead and made cars for their boys. Ryan made his own.

On the day of the race, Ryan showed up with his clunker, and he looked around and saw the other boys with their sleek cars that had been engineered by their fathers.

In the race, Ryan's car finished last. Dead last. That pretty much said it all about how his boyhood was going.

At school, Ryan was failing to turn in his homework assignments, and he was piling up plenty of demerits.

His mother and I got a call from the school. They needed us to come for a conference.

He shouldn't be here, they told us. *He needs to be somewhere he can be challenged.*

They shared with us the results of a standardized test. Ryan's score, they were stunned to learn, was among the highest scores in the history of the school.

We ended up moving to New Jersey. Ryan and Kelly were accepted to the prestigious and highly selective Princeton Day School.

For the first time in his life, Ryan was intellectually challenged, surrounded by like-minded kids and respected for his intellectual horsepower.

He had been at the school for a mere week when he turned to me and said:

Dad, I feel like I've found my home.

I still can't tell that story without shedding a tear or two.

I belong here.

He sure did.

Ryan would go on to graduate as one of the top students in the class. He went off to Haverford College where he served as the student representative to the Board of Trustees. After graduation, he lived a few years in New York City, where he worked a stint at the *Paris Review*, and then made his way to the Ph.D. program in 18th Century American Literature at Yale.

My daughter, Kelly, was a scholar, too, sailing through Princeton Day and serving on the Teen Council. She gained acceptance to Skidmore College, where she was chair of the

Integrity Board, and did well enough to get into law school at the University of New Hampshire. She's now the lawyer in the family.

I saw up close what Princeton Day could do. It attracted students who were extremely smart—and parents who were extremely affluent.

When the kids started at Princeton Day, I was possibly the poorest dad on campus. More than once, I had to swallow my pride and call the school to ask for more time to pay the tuition bill.

Princeton Day School, a stately brick institution located on a street fittingly named, Great Road, had long catered to the children of privilege. Its students over the years included Christopher Reeve, the late Superman star, who was the grandson of Prudential Financial CEO, Colonel Richard Henry Reeve, as well as a descendant of John Winthrop, the governor of the Massachusetts Bay Colony. Reeve had some other Mayflower kin, and a couple of Supreme Court justices in his brood, too.

Those were the kinds of pedigrees that got tossed around at Princeton Day.

This was a school with a planetarium, an architectural studio, an ice rink, six fields for lacrosse and field hockey, indoor and outdoor amphitheaters, and a music facility with seven soundproof rehearsal rooms. For field trips, students at Princeton Day might venture to Europe or China.

My business was doing okay at the time. But in the rarefied atmosphere at Princeton Day, my children felt almost like poor kids.

When Heartland achieved significant success, and went public in 2005, I no longer needed to call the school to talk about my tuition balance.

Now they were calling me.

When the school launched a fundraising drive, a leader of the campaign approached me to ask for a contribution of $500,000. I said I'd think about it, and went home to discuss it with my family.

The kids offered an idea. They said kids at Princeton Day already had just about everything—except some poor and working-class classmates. Kids who struggled economically could bring some wisdom and experience that most students at PDS didn't possess: what it was like to do without.

My daughter, Emmalee, in fact, passed on Princeton Day for high school, instead choosing a progressive boarding school with a working dairy farm, in large part because she bristled at the elitism and the culture of materialism. She had already attended Princeton Day for ten years, from junior kindergarten through eighth grade. She wanted something different for her high school years.

· · ·

I went back to the leader of the fundraising campaign and offered a proposition:

You asked for $500,000. How would you like $11 million?

They offered to name the new building after me.

I passed.

But I had a different agenda. The money had to go to pay for tuition for poor and working-class children of any racial background.

By this time, I was a member of the Board of Trustees and I was invited to explain my proposal.

One of the board members asked about using the money to create partial scholarships. That way, parents might pay only half-tuition.

That missed the point. When this program started in 2006, it would cost $320,000 to send a kid from junior kindergarten through senior year of high school at Princeton Day. Even 5 percent of that would be a boatload of money beyond the wildest dreams of working-class people.

I told them that I was talking about recruiting students who would have absolutely no chance—zero possibility—of coming to Princeton Day without a full scholarship.

And so it began. The admissions office spread word to other schools in New Jersey about this new scholarship program. We soon learned that a promotional campaign wasn't necessary. When one of the nation's most prestigious day schools starts offering full scholarships, word gets around.

The scholarship included full tuition, as well as the cost for books, supplies and daily lunch. The kids would also receive funding to take the class trips to faraway destinations, as well as daily transportation to and from school.

We funded a position for a counselor who would be there to help the scholarship kids and their families manage the many details—like taking the bus from a poor neighborhood in Trenton—that would be new to them.

The first of the *Give Something Back Foundation* scholars arrived in the 2006–2007 school year. Since then, more than fifty deserving students have attended the school, changing its complexion, quite literally. As Paul Stellato, the head of school put it, *It has been a transformation.*

. . .

As an eighth-grader, Dennis Cannon had applied to Princeton Day on a lark. He was plenty bright and talented, a star on both the middle school math squad and the sports teams.

But he was a lower-middle-class kid, and he knew that Princeton Day was way out of reach for families like his. He lived with a single mom, Tara, who struggled from paycheck to paycheck, and a younger sister, Caitlin. His mom would never say how much she earned. She was embarrassed. She was afraid the kids might mention the paltry sum to their friends.

The family had lived for several years in a dismal apartment complex after the divorce. They were able to afford to move to a modest house during Dennis' middle school years, when his grandfather moved in and helped with expenses. But there was certainly no money for a private school, not to speak of a prestigious institution like Princeton Day. Dennis had no idea about any scholarship program.

He filled out the application, he later recalled, not because he had any intention of going to Princeton Day. He just wanted to see if he measured up academically to the smart rich kids. If he wasn't *wealthy enough* to attend Princeton Day, he might at least have the satisfaction of knowing he was *smart enough* to hang with the elite.

And he would have an acceptance letter to prove it.

It was a kind of a game, and a long shot at that. But as the notification date grew near, Dennis found himself deeply invested in this gambit. When the bus dropped him off after school, he would run to the mailbox to see if an envelope from Princeton Day had arrived.

And then one Saturday afternoon in the spring of 2006, Dennis arrived home from baseball practice. He was standing outside with his mother when the mail arrived. They opened the box.

There it was—a big packet from Princeton Day.

He knew a thick envelope was a good sign.

His mother excitedly ripped it open as Dennis stood behind her, reading over her shoulder.

Congratulations, the first sentence began, *you have been accepted to the class of 2010...*

Dennis stopped reading. He had won his game, even if it really didn't mean anything.

His mom kept reading. The second paragraph delivered the shocker. Dennis had been chosen as a *Give Something Back Foundation* scholar. He was being given a financial award that would pay for tuition.

She broke down in sobs, unable to speak for some moments. Dennis looked more closely at the letter and saw the big numbers after the dollar sign.

His mother turned and wrapped her arms around him.

You deserve this, she whispered to her son.

Dennis remembers going limp, so shell-shocked he couldn't even summon the strength to hug her back at first.

A few years later, his sister, Caitlin, would win a scholarship, too.

When his school year started, a couple of things became very evident to Dennis: *These kids wear some really nice clothes. And man, the classes are tough.*

The student-teacher ratio was 8 to 1. You couldn't hide in the back of the room, zone out, and be left alone. Everyone was expected to contribute. If you hadn't done your homework, Dennis learned, it was obvious to the teacher and everyone else. And it was not acceptable.

Among the school officials, there might have been some questions about whether the scholars from modest backgrounds would be able to adjust to these demanding environs.

They did more than that. They became leaders.

In his sophomore year, Dennis was elected vice president of the class. As a junior, he was captain of the football team. As a senior, he was captain of the baseball team.

He became president of the Athletic Association, which promoted school spirit. He joined an organization called Youth for the Elderly, which spent hours every Sunday visiting the lonely residents of homes for the aged in the Princeton area.

Dennis was a kid with charisma, and a top athlete, to boot, so it was little surprise that he became a popular figure in this wealthy crowd. He would have been a star anywhere.

In a quiet, informal way, he became a mentor to the scholarship kids who came after him, especially those who worried about whether they could truly fit in this kind of a world.

The thing we had in common was financial instability, he recalled, *and that was something the upper-class kids couldn't really understand.*

Riding the bus to school, for example, seemed a foreign concept to most of the wealthy students.

Why wouldn't your mom drive you?

Or your nanny?

If you were one of *the kids without nice clothes*, as Dennis put it, you could feel more than a little insecure. Some of the snobbier kids would occasionally make fun behind another kid's back.

Dennis remembers one group chortling about the clothes worn by a scholarship student, a girl from a rough, inner-city neighborhood of Trenton.

As they were making cracks about her fashion tastes, Dennis wheeled and shot them a glare.

Hey, knock it off, he barked. *She can dress any way she wants to.*

Dennis didn't think the kids meant to be cruel. They just didn't understand. When you grow up in a certain style, he said, you think everyone is born with designer clothes hanging in the closet.

He helped boost another poor young girl, a kid who rose at dawn to catch the bus, and fought to maintain her energy through the school day. She confided to Dennis about her worries. She wasn't sure she had the talent to succeed at Princeton Day.

He set her straight.

You already have succeeded, he told her. *You get up at 5 a.m. to catch a bus! You use your strength to fight your way through. And you are smart. Don't doubt that.*

After graduating from Princeton Day, and turning down baseball offers from Division III schools, Dennis went to the University of Miami. He is now an accountant for a downtown Miami firm, and he is working on his master's degree and the Certified Public Accountant exam.

The biggest thing Princeton Day did for me, by far, was inspire me to step out of my boundaries, he said. *It created this motivation in me that I can do anything.*

. . .

Darling Cerna was five years old when her family moved to the United States from Guatemala.

She learned to speak English as a kindergartener. She remembers it being one of the hardest things she has ever done. The only thing harder, she said, was watching her parents go through the same struggle to express themselves.

Her parents worked at a country club. Her dad was a waiter. Her mom worked in the maintenance department.

My dad serves and my mom cleans, said Darling.

When she came to Princeton Day for the first time, she remembers thinking the place looked like something out of a fairy tale. The buildings were beautiful. The students were fashionable. There were no metal detectors. There weren't even any locks on the lockers.

She joined the school in the seventh grade. She was the only Latina in the class. There was a single Latino boy.

I'm a little different than most of the students here, she noticed, and not just because of the shade of her skin. *They're all wearing Sperrys. They could buy anything they wanted. We'd have a break at Thanksgiving, and these kids would go to Cancun or the Bahamas.*

For a while, Darling wasn't sure she could compete intellectually with her new peers at Princeton Day.

I wondered if I should be here, she remembers. *These kids are smart. And not just in class, but in the way they talk. And they're so confident in themselves.*

In seventh and eighth grade, she got some Bs. For a girl who had been accustomed to getting all As—and for parents accustomed to the top grades, too—it caused some major disappointment.

As she started high school, however, it began to dawn on Darling that while she might be getting financial help to attend Princeton Day, she didn't lack for brainpower.

Something inside told me, 'You can do this.'

She kicked it into high gear.

When grades were handed out at the end of the trimester, Darling, like the other students, was called in to meet with an advisor, who showed the marks for each class, along with teacher comments.

With her heart beating, Darling looked and saw 'A,' 'A,' 'A,' 'A,' 'A.'

And then she read the teacher comments.

Darling comes to class well-prepared...

Darling always has a positive attitude...

Darling wrote this wonderful essay...

Her heart was singing.

As she stood in the hallway, Darling could hear grousing among many of her fellow students, disappointed in their grades.

Careful not to gloat, she stayed calm and quiet as she texted her dad to tell him the news about her marks.

I'll never forget that moment, she later recalled. I thought, *'Wow—I am up to par with these kids!'*

In her senior year, Darling was honored with the John Douglas Sacks-Wilner Award for resolution, courage and self-command, and a distinguished commitment to excellence.

Darling is now a pre-med student at Muhlenberg College, a highly regarded liberal arts school in Pennsylvania. She hopes to become a pediatrician.

. . .

The medical field will also need to make room for Josiah Meekins, a senior at Princeton Day who plans to become a dentist.

Josiah—named for a boy in the Bible who became a king at age 11—sometimes gets a bit of affectionate teasing about his fancy school from his friends back at home in Lawrence, New Jersey.

The other kids talk about *mixing it up* and *throwing down*.

He told his pals there were no fistfights at Princeton Day.

No fighting? one friend asked incredulously. *Man, you're not in the 'hood!*

He laughed along with his friends.

I'm a lover, not a fighter, Josiah told them.

His friends cracked up.

They like to give me a hard time about 'going to that fancy white school,' he said. *But at the end of the day, we're all good friends.*

Princeton Day has become a family tradition. His older brother, Joshua, twenty-one, went to the school. He recently graduated from Villanova. His younger brother, Jomar, twelve, is a sixth-grader at Princeton Day.

Josiah, an African American, is the co-chair of the school's Black Latino Student Union, a group that meets in a classroom on Thursdays to share stories and occasionally vent about stereotypes.

Growing up in a family with strong Christian beliefs, Josiah attends the Union Baptist Church every Sunday, where services start at 9:30 a.m. and sometimes stretch past noon. *It's a long time in the pews, but worth it,* he says, *to learn more about the Word of God.*

At Princeton Day, Josiah is a member of HITOPS—Health Interested Teens Own Program on Sexuality. The group of students visits other schools, as well as juvenile detention facilities, to talk to young students about things like sex, drugs and homophobia.

A lot of people who grew up in Christian families are taught not to accept gays, he said. *In HITOPS, we don't try to tell people what to think. We just give them information, and encourage them to listen to other people's ideas.*

As a Bible believer himself, Josiah knows his Leviticus and the admonition against men lying with men. He also believes the book *was written for a different time.*

I believe God is accepting of gay people, Josiah said. *God accepts everyone.*

A tennis player for Princeton Day, Josiah volunteers as an instructor on the courts for kids in poorer neighborhoods. He hopes to teach them about more than tennis.

One of his tennis students, a little girl named Lea, told Josiah about her passion for reading. He saw that Lea was a very smart girl, the kind of kid who would relish academic rigor.

Josiah went to the girl's father and told him about Princeton Day.

I do want my daughter to be challenged, the dad told Josiah.

The family looked into it and made an application. Lea won admission and a scholarship. She is now in the second grade. By all accounts, the smart little girl has a world of promise in her eyes.

And one thing is for certain: This rich kid school is just a little bit richer for having Lea, a little girl from Trenton with some big dreams, as one of its students.

17

SURVIVORS AND SCHOLARS

———————◆———————

When Gabriela Bogatz was four years old, and her screaming father would fly into a violent rage, the little girl would scoop up her baby sister, Klaudia, and flee to a bedroom, where they hid behind a locked door.

If she could hear the sounds of her dad hitting her mom, Gabriela would call the police. When she tried to step in and protect her mom, she was slapped around.

Gabriela's parents, who were born in Poland, split when she was six years old. Her mother, Gosia, supported the kids by working long hours as a house cleaner, and so it fell to Gabriela to care for her sister.

Starting in the first grade, Gabriela did the cooking. She did the cleaning. She and her sister were not allowed to go outside and play, and no friends could come over, because it was supposed to be a secret that the little girls were home alone.

When she reached high school, and her sister was old enough to fend for herself, Gabriela took a job as a waitress at the

Diamond Family Restaurant in Joliet to help pay the bills at home.

Without a car, she would depend on friends for rides to work. Gabriela was a teenager without an iPhone, an iPad, a computer. The only television at home was in her mom's room.

Gabriela and Klaudia wore clothes that had been given to their mom by the people who lived in the houses she cleaned.

At Lockport High School, Gabriela takes Advanced Placement classes in English and history. She is a volunteer in the attendance office. She serves as a school ambassador, greeting newcomers and looking out for any students who seem to be invisible to their peers.

Gabriella is a scholar in English, but her first language is Polish, which she can still speak, read and write. She is also fluent in Spanish, and she can converse in Slovak and Ukrainian.

For all of her scholarly talents, she knew the cold facts from an early age: If she was going to go to college, she would have to figure out how to pay for it.

On the day that Gabriela learned that she had won a *Give Something Back Foundation* scholarship, the teenager and her mother hugged and danced and wept.

You're going to college, her mom proclaimed.

I am going to college, Gabriela responded through her tears.

Her sister, Klaudia, shouted in celebration with them.

Gabriela gathered up $100 of her savings from work and went to Holy Cross Catholic Church in Joliet, where she attends Mass every Sunday. From a pew, she knelt and gave thanks for her scholarship. And she donated the $100 to a church mission that helps poor children in other countries.

Gabriela will enroll in college in the fall of 2015. She wants to study psychology. As she put it, there's a lot we don't understand about *the chemistry of the brain* and *the way it makes people act.*

She is looking forward to the collegiate atmosphere, being just another student on campus, hanging out and having a social life. *I had to grow up pretty fast,* she said, *so I never really knew much about being a kid.*

.   .   .

Each year, I host a dinner banquet for the scholarship winners and the others in our foundation. In my remarks, I tell the young people about my background, which in many ways is like their own, with a scarcity of money and perhaps some family troubles.

I talk about my long-ago gift from the Lockport Woman's Club. I tell them about my business success, how I worked hard, but how I was also fortunate to be in the right place at the right time.

I got a break, I tell the scholarship winners, *and now you've gotten a break, too.*

As I look out at the crowd, a sea of young faces of many colors and backgrounds, I urge them to follow their dreams and, if they can, to give something back someday.

.   .   .

When Tariq Pinnick was a little boy, he marveled at how his father, Richard, would go out of his way to tell an impoverished and elderly woman how beautiful she looked in her Sunday dress, knowing it might have been some time since she had received a compliment from anyone.

He watched his dad walk up to a homeless man in Chicago who was searching for food in a dumpster, and invite him to join them at a restaurant for a good hot meal.

Tariq would tell his father: *You like to put a smile on people's faces. There are not many dads like you.*

Tariq and his brother, Terrell, grew up in a house without much money. But his dad showed them the value of a moral compass.

Richard Pinnick has raised his boys as a single dad since the kids were three and five. *Since they were growing up without a mother,* Richard said, *I had to remember that they were going to need hugs and kisses, and that it was up to me to give them those hugs and kisses.*

He taught them that being an African American male means toeing the line and watching your step, however unfair that might sometimes seem.

It's not like the white knights are riding through the streets, Richard said, *but you can't help notice that an awful lot of black kids around here get arrested for a pretty minor thing, and then there's a blot on their record that makes it hard for them to get a job.*

He is careful to resist bitterness. As a black man, and a United States Army veteran, he once took pity on a neo-Nazi who called him a racial slur.

You're better than that, he told the man. *We got to talking. Turns out this guy had done some time in prison, and that's where he got mixed up in this racist nonsense. By the end of it, he was crying on my shoulder.*

As a father, Richard has instilled in his sons the importance of school work above social life and extracurricular activities. Tariq worked part-time at a fast-food restaurant, but otherwise pored over his schoolwork at the kitchen table. His father kept watch.

Plenty of kids can play sports, he told his sons. *Stick to the books.*

He worried, though, that the costs of a university were beyond reach.

When Tariq told him about the foundation scholarships, Richard thought there was a misunderstanding, or that his son had been the victim of some cruel joke.

They pay 100 percent of college costs? the dad asked. *Yeah, right.*

Richard says he is now the only man in his economically struggling circle of friends who can boast about a son going to a university.

My son, the college student, he proudly noted.

When Tariq won a scholarship to attend Lewis University, he said his dad hugged him very tightly and told him about the responsibilities that go with being given a gift.

I'm going to work hard, said Tariq. *I want so much to make my dad proud.*

. . .

Guadalupe Flores knew other first-generation Hispanic kids, especially girls, whose parents were fearful about allowing them to move away for college.

My best friend is really smart, she said, *and she couldn't go.*

When Guadalupe won a scholarship, her parents struggled for a bit with the idea, but let her follow her dreams to Bradley University in Peoria, even though it seemed like a world away.

Guadalupe had already risen to challenges that were far more difficult. At fifteen, when her mom was diagnosed with cancer, Guadalupe had started taking over a lot of parental roles, such as writing checks for household bills and running errands.

Her mom died at forty-six. Guadalupe was seventeen.

Before she passed away, she told me she was very proud of me and she wanted me to realize my dreams, said Guadalupe. *She told me not to take on too big of a load at home. She said the family will be okay. You need to be a kid.*

Guadalupe, who is studying nursing in pediatric oncology, has been a leader at Bradley, especially when it comes to helping other Hispanic students find their way in the culture of rural Illinois.

At school, you might encounter someone who has never even met a Mexican before, she said.

She said Hispanic students can feel embarrassed around others about their customs, music or food. Guadalupe remembers an Anglo roommate who recoiled at her eating a favorite Mexican delicacy of cow tongue.

I was honored that Guadalupe remembered some advice I had given to the scholarship winners about them being special. I had encouraged the kids to see their challenges as sources of strength.

And that's what Guadalupe has done.

She volunteers at Friendship House, a resource in Peoria for the Hispanic community, serving many people who do not speak English. She serves as a mentor with the Girl Scouts. She is president of the Association of Latin American Students at Bradley.

I know that my mom would be very proud of me, she said.

A lot of us are proud of Guadalupe.

. . .

Nicole Barker was a freshman at Eastern Illinois University when she lost her father, Dennis, to colon cancer.

Unable to think about much besides her dad, a powerfully built bricklayer who died at forty-nine, she let her school work slide. It can be tough to focus on an essay about the Charles Dickens novel, *Great Expectations*, when you've lost your father.

As one of our scholarship winners, Nicole's marks were regularly sent to us, and so we were alerted that her grades had suddenly fallen.

Nicole received a letter from the foundation offering her encouragement and help, but reminding her that she needed to pull up her grades to keep the scholarship.

Nicole would later say that the letter was even more important to her than the scholarship money.

It's one thing to write a check, she said. *It's another to know that someone has high expectations for you—and that you need to be accountable.*

Years later, she sent a letter of gratitude about the encouragement that is worth more to me than gold.

It was a pivotal point in my life, and I could choose to give up, lose the scholarship, she wrote, *or fight with everything I've got to get through it. Someone believes you're worth it—prove it!!!*

She might have *just slipped away*, as she put it, and given up on college and her hopes of a fulfilling career. Instead, she pulled herself up. She hit the books.

Nicole, who is in her late twenties, is now a successful chemist.

. . .

Adrianna Martinez was fourteen years old when she gave birth in 2012. Little Ian arrived during the second semester of Adrianna's freshman year at Lockport High School.

My mom had been a teen mother, said Adrianna, who is now a sixteen-year-old junior. *She had hoped I would break the cycle and find a way to go to college.*

Her working-class parents were barely managing to keep the bills paid. To make things even more difficult, her mom and dad were helping out their own parents with money.

Adrianna had always been a very bright girl with a shining star in her future. But now it seemed that everything had changed.

Many of her friends fell away. Some of them had parents who were disapproving. Others simply didn't want to hang socially with somebody carrying a crying baby.

Even at the church she attended, she said, her family felt as though they were being treated as outcasts.

And where in the world would they find money for college?

In the fall of 2013, a letter arrived at the Martinez home. Adrianna had been awarded a *Give Something Back* scholarship. As with all of the recipients, she would need to demonstrate exemplary character and continue to meet high academic goals.

She isn't wasting her chance. Adrianna has taken Advanced Placement courses in chemistry, United States history, biology and French.

Her mom's side of the family is Mexican American. Her dad's side came from Puerto Rico. They have been Illinoisans for generations. No Spanish was spoken in Adrianna's home.

Still, some relatives asked, *Why French and not Spanish? Because I like French,* she replied.

In the spring of 2014, Adrianna prepared to take the ACT, the college entrance exam. She had been taking practice tests over and over. She wanted to prove that she was strong enough to climb steep hills, and smart enough to compete with students who had more advantages.

She hopes to study marine biology at a university.

When the ACT score came in the mail, she and her mother could hardly believe what they were seeing.

Adrianna had scored a 31. That placed her in the 97th percentile.

I was jumping for joy, Adrianna recalled, *and my mom was jumping, too.*

There were surely some people who bet against her when she had a baby at such a young age.

I'm betting on Adrianna.

. . .

Evicted from their home, Shannon Stoffey and her mom bounced around among relatives for about a year. Aunts and uncles took turns giving them shelter. For a long stretch, they stayed in the basement of the homes of friends.

Throughout her school years, Shannon did without a computer at home. It would have been a luxury out of the reach of her mother, Karen, who worked long hours as a cashier at a gas station.

After winning her scholarship, Shannon attended the University of Illinois. Like me many years before, she had never set foot on the campus before she enrolled. Compared to classmates on campus, her clothes were modest.

Her grades, on the other hand, were dazzling. She would go on to become a lawyer.

She continued to volunteer for the *Give Something Back Foundation*. She served as a mentor. She took girls living with hardships to the bowling alley, attended dance recitals, and acted as a chaperone on college visits.

When one teenager was wavering about going away to school, worried about leaving her boyfriend, Shannon counseled that *A relationship shouldn't stand in the way of college.*

One of her mentees anguished about the fighting in public between her separated parents, and Shannon was able to offer encouragement and share that the split between her mom and dad was similarly *less than amicable.*

In helping other kids who have climbed steep hills, Shannon is truly giving back.

The foundation is my family, she says.

When I first met Shannon, I was surprised to learn that this high school kid and her mom were living in a complex called the Lockport South Apartments. It was the same dreary, sad complex where I had lived so long ago, after a failed first marriage, at a time I was struggling to find a way to pay the bills.

When she found out where I had lived, Shannon would later recall thinking: *He is one of us.*

I am honored to be in such company.

Now successful in her law practice, Shannon recently bought a house of her own. Her new place is a short walk, if a world away, from that old apartment complex where she—and I, so many years before her—knew the weight of struggle. She can practically see the old apartment complex.

For working-class kids like Shannon Stoffey—and Bob Carr—who are lucky enough to catch a break and achieve some measure of prosperity, it is good to be able to see the way home.

18

THE STUFF THAT MATTERS

On Valentine's Day in 2006, Jill and I and our kids moved into a second home, a soothing, sun-dappled and lushly wooded place on Lake Sunapee in New Hampshire.

At the lake house, the kids would play games of leaping off the boat while trying to catch tennis balls that were hurled into the air. The dogs would chase the kids into the water, and the ducks would chase the dogs, a circus of splashes and giggles and barking.

We drank wine at the harbor and treated ourselves to ice cream at Bubba's. We hosted big dinner parties, especially during summer, those glorious days with cool New England breezes and evenings of watching the sun melt gently into the lake.

And then it grew pitch black, the pure darkness you never know in urban areas. We'd play bocce with a glow-in-the-dark ball that had been given to us by Sue and her wife, Anne, colleagues and dear friends who live nearby. And we told stories and we laughed.

The lake house stood for peace, and then later, after the fateful lightning bolt, it would signify promise.

Like the Princeton house, the place at the lake was tended by Ben Hill. As a boy of three, Ben had come with his family to New Jersey from England. Growing up, Ben had struggled in school with dyslexia. He never gave much thought to going to college. He was still searching for his true vocation and role in life in 1992, when I hired him as a carpenter to build some computer desks for the kids.

I discovered that he had worked as a chef before becoming a carpenter. This was a man of many talents. I eventually hired him as our full-time manager in charge of the things I didn't have the time—or the skills—to do myself. It's a pretty long list.

Ben lives in Andover, about ten miles from our lake house, with his bride, Amy. They had been sweethearts through high school in the 1970s and beyond. Amy had tired of waiting for a marriage proposal, and ventured off in a direction on her own. Many years later, after a marriage and kids and a divorce, she found her way back to Ben, who had remained single all those years.

Uncle Ben, as he is known to my kids, will always be a member of our family. Ben, whose pony tail is now flecked with a bit of gray, manages to put up with me and takes very good care of us.

It was Ben's voice on the line when the phone rang at 4 a.m. on July 2, 2014.

I have some very bad news, he told me in a heavy voice. *Your house has burned down.*

A lightning bolt had apparently hit my copper chimney and ignited a furious blaze. With winds whipping at about twenty-five miles per hour, the fire spread fast. The alarm company called the house at 2:07 a.m. but got no answer. They called Ben soon after that. By the time he arrived at 2:30 a.m., the house was in full roar. An hour later, little remained but ashes.

For the next two hours, I sat in my bed in the Princeton house and thought: *Now what?*

I knew I was a lucky man. No one had died. No one was injured.

My daughter, Kelly, had been planning to drive to New Hampshire early that very week, but was stalled in Chicago by car troubles.

I could easily have been in the house. I had made plans to be at the place July 1 through the Fourth, working with the co-author of this book, Dirk Johnson. But just a week or so before our meeting, we postponed our plans. It was highly unusual that no one was staying in the house in the first week of July. It was also a monumental stroke of good fortune. Anyone sleeping in the bedrooms upstairs would likely have perished.

At 6 a.m., I sent a text to several members of my family and some friends, telling them what had happened.

Jill immediately called me from her apartment in New York City. She was heartsick.

With the divorce, the beloved lake house had vanished from her life. It had been an almost magical place for her. When she left me, it had pained her deeply to lose her connection to the home and Lake Sunapee. She had not been back to the lake since we agreed to part more than three years earlier.

I want to see it, she told me over the phone. *Please let me go with you.*

On our ride to New Hampshire, Jill was in tears.

As we pulled near the lake house, we could see police tape at the driveway. We got out of the car and saw our friends, Sue and Anne, come running toward us. They had been crying.

The place was gone. The surrounding trees were brown. Many of them would surely die.

Many treasured items were burned in the fire. The collection of watercolors painted by my grandmother had been on display there. I lost my diplomas from the University of Illinois. Gone was the autobiography I had written at the age of twelve. I lost my sports varsity letters from high school. And the old *New York Times* newspaper from 1971, with the classified ad announcing my presidential bid, went up in flames, too.

Holly had just given me a large afghan that she had knitted for me. It was beautifully crafted with different shades of brown eventually turning into pure white. It had brought back heartfelt memories. Corrie had long ago given me a needlepoint poem that meant the world to me.

Over the next days and weeks, I would receive hundreds of emails and calls from people. They were all feeling sorry for me, as though this was a terrible tragedy.

I did not shed a tear. *It was all just stuff.*

In the wake of the fire, to be candid, I felt a sense of liberation. Material possessions can weigh a person down. Less is often best.

For years, I had assumed I'd be going to the lake house for the rest of my days. The routine of my future was set. I had figured I would die there.

After the fire, it struck me that I was no longer tied to the place, as wonderful as it had been, and that I could chart new courses. As the young man that I am—a youngster of only sixty-eight—I was now free to do anything I wanted. I could spend a winter in Barbados, a summer in Sweden, return to the Seychelles Islands or Bali, or even Bora Bora.

Some of the kids are talking about buying the land from me. And the insurance company cut a check for the house.

All of the money is going to the foundation, every last penny. I did the math. It translated to full-ride scholarships for another 280 students. With the house in Princeton already pledged to the foundation in my will, I believe that my goal of putting 1,000 kids through college is now achievable, with more work yet to be done.

Who knows where the next adventure will take me. It might seem odd for a man to be so upbeat after a blaze has destroyed his beautiful lake house. But it thrills me to know that more poor and working-class students, kids facing some of the challenges I once knew, will now go to college.

Rising above hardship and adversity, these are young people who are going to make a difference. They're going to set the world on fire.

ROBERT OWEN CARR

AFTERWORD

We live in a world of profound complexity. There is much to be discouraged about, but also plenty of reasons for optimism. The young people of today who are struggling to get *out of the woods* will soon lead the world and run its great economic engines.

This gives me much hope. I sit in a position to see so many opportunities ahead for entrepreneurs who seek to make this world a better place. If there has ever been a better time to break out on your own and forge change in the world, I don't know when that would have been.

Today's American middle class is struggling to improve its standard of living. Around the world, too, there are daunting problems, but also great successes. In recent decades, the woes of poverty and overpopulation have improved dramatically. In too many places, including America, corruption still stands in the way of prosperity for many.

I wish I could have written a more positive book about capitalism in America today. But I am calling it as I see it and live it every day. I believe that those of us who are privileged with the power to effect change have the responsibility to do the right thing and to call for a high level of ethical behavior.

We can be so much better than we are today. More people of goodwill need to speak out and stop tolerating the criminal and almost criminal behaviors that we witness and have learned to live with and thereby encourage.

Fortunately, there are many who truly want to do the right thing, even when the right thing might not be the most profitable. But many others yield to the temptation to sacrifice principles for profit. Good people who stick their heads in the sand are not helping.

We can reduce the actions of the few who harm the many by holding people responsible. We must refuse to accept unfair and deceptive business practices. It is important that we raise our voices, rather than look the other way.

I want to believe that goodwill and honorable deeds eventually do triumph. About 155 years ago, a lanky fifty-one-year-old man who had never experienced much worldly success, was en route to visiting his son in New Hampshire. He stopped in New York to give a speech.

In what was to become his famous Cooper Union speech, Abraham Lincoln ended with the statement that would make him the next president of the United States. Those words were: *Let us have faith that right makes might....* Within a few years, those words and this great man changed the world for the better, freeing millions of slaves and allowing the rest of the world to lift its head higher.

Principles stand the test of the ages. The importance of ethics holds for presidents and for everyone else, too, like Mary Frances Carr, for instance, who simply believed in doing the right thing. *~roc*

INDEX